THE MODERN NATIONS IN HISTORICAL PERSPECTIVE

ROBIN W. WINKS, *General Editor*

The volumes in this series deal with individual nations or groups of closely related nations throughout the world, summarizing the chief historical trends and influences that have contributed to each nation's present-day character, problems, and behavior. Recent data are incorporated with established historical background to achieve a fresh synthesis and original interpretation.

The author of this volume, MARIO RODRÍGUEZ, received his Ph.D. from the University of California, Berkeley. He is now Professor of History at the University of Arizona, but has spent much time recently in Guatemala City, Central America, on a Guggenheim Fellowship (1964-1965). He was granted a Morse Fellowship in History (1958-1959) and awarded the James Alexander Robertson Prize of the Conference of Latin American History (1955). A contributing editor of the *Handbook of Latin American Studies*, Professor Rodríguez has also published A *Palmerstonian Diplomat in Central America—Frederick Chatfield, Esq.*, and numerous articles in the field of Latin and Central American studies.

CENTRAL AMERICA

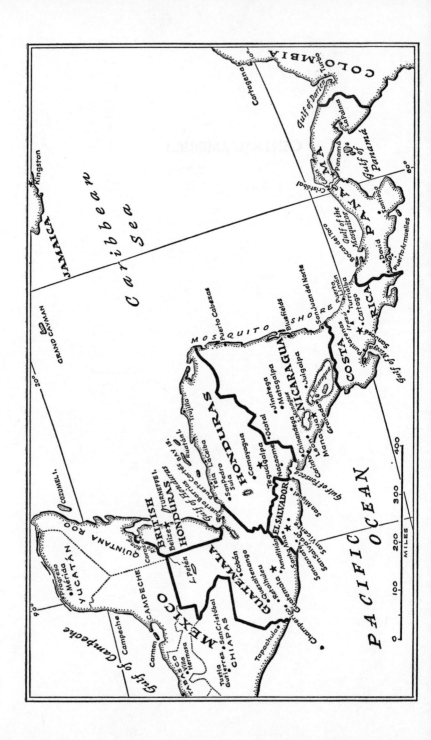

CENTRAL AMERICA

MARIO RODRÍGUEZ

A SPECTRUM BOOK

Prentice-Hall, Inc.

Englewood Cliffs, New Jersey

Current printing (last digit):

11   10   9   8   7   6   5   4   3   2

P 12239, C 12240

To the memory of
John Fitzgerald Kennedy

In the classroom, the historian frequently generalizes, almost to the danger point, to give his students a meaningful picture of national developments while implanting in their minds an appreciation for the complexity of certain issues and problems so that they will learn to be more critical in forming their judgment and be able to see through facile evaluations of a given event or period. Drawing from his own research experience, as well as years of mulling over the literature and conclusions of fellow practitioners, he finally arrives at the synthesis which he presents in his lectures. When it comes to putting this interpretation on paper, however, that same outspoken historian is a model of caution, afraid of *el quedirán* ("What will they say?"), as the Spaniards call it. Professor F. S. C. Northrop of Yale University once told me (and I shall paraphrase him rather loosely): "The trouble with you historians is that you always reach the side of the river but you are afraid to jump." Given the conviviality of the occasion, I retorted that there was no point in jumping if you were going to fall into the water and drown. Apparently, I was not completely satisfied with the answer I gave the famous philosopher. In these interpretive essays I have decided to jump, hoping to reach the opposite bank.

Furthermore, and since the distance is a long one, I felt it wise to be as unencumbered as possible; footnoting every clause and explaining my reasons for making every statement would have involved a second book and would have defeated the purposes of this series. I have, therefore, limited the number of footnotes; the bibliographical essay gives the major English references that I have consulted; the Central American items are not included—again, because of the nature of this series. Neverthe-less, I humbly thank all the authors whose works I have gleaned for this survey. I am especially thankful for the *Hispanic American Report* in writing about the contemporary scene.

An author is always indebted to persons and institutions for their services and contributions to the final product even though the ultimate responsibility for the work is his. Thanks to the University of Arizona, I was able to exploit the research talents of Vincent C. Peloso, who did an excellent job of studying the themes of "Nationalism" and "Union-ism" from World War II to the present. Professors Wayne M. Clegern and Louis E. Bumgartner served as convenient sounding boards for some of my views; Professor J. Joaquín Pardo, Director of the Archives in Guatemala City—whose death in early August 1964 deprived Central American scholars of a valuable ally—gave me some insights into Gua-temalan politics from Ubico's time to the present; and many others, including especially Juanita White, Concha Orantes, Bertlyn Bosley, Arturo Taracena, Werner Ascoli, and Guillermo Arroyave. My wife Mildred and daughter Jacqueline likewise did their yeoman share of the work. *Gracias a todos.*

M. R.

CONTENTS

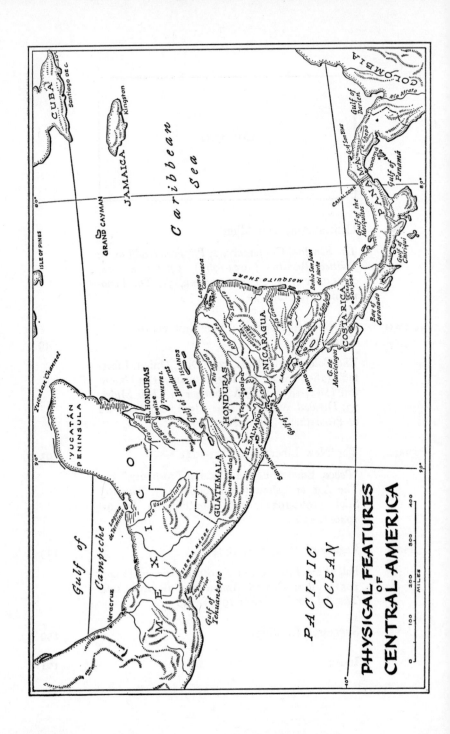

PHYSICAL FEATURES
OF
CENTRAL AMERICA

ONE

CENTRAL AMERICAN ALLIES

We will build a wall around Cuba—not a wall
of mortar or brick or barbed wire, but a wall of
dedicated men determined to protect their own
freedom and sovereignty.[1]

John Fitzgerald Kennedy, March 18, 1963

Scarcely a few weeks before the Bay of Pigs fiasco of
April 1961, the United States government announced a special aid
program for Latin America, the Alliance for Progress, which Latin
Americans of varying political persuasions have since come to eye
with suspicion. Conservatives in the more "traditional" or less advanced nations can hardly be expected to welcome eagerly a policy
and a course of action that proposes to undermine the long-standing
supremacy of their class. At the other end of the political spectrum,
Communists and Castroites view the *Alianza para el Progreso* as
another "neocolonialist" scheme in the imperialist's bag of tricks.
Even moderates, who ordinarily might be counted on to support this
program of gradual and rational social change, have doubts concerning the sincerity of the American people in advancing these reforms.
After all, at the time of the Chapultepec Conference of early 1945
and ever since, the United States had been reluctant to accept a
similar program outlined by the Latins themselves. If the Northern

[1] As quoted in the New York *Times* (Western Ed.), March 19, 1963.

1

republic was now willing to adopt these suggestions merely in response to Fidel Castro, what would happen once the bearded premier no longer held sway on his Caribbean isle? Conceivably, they reasoned, the United States might then drop the *Alianza* altogether, embarrassing its supporters throughout Latin America and making their political position untenable. Local rivals could effectively label them "puppets" who had been used and then abandoned by their Northern benefactor.

Despite these misgivings about the intentions of the United States, many Latin Americans were hopeful that President Kennedy, the author and champion of the new *Alianza*, might successfully lead his people into another Good Neighbor era, one which would help to satisfy the national aspirations of Latin Americans while at the same time protecting the Western Hemisphere, in a realistic manner, from the challenge of *Fidelismo*. The unfortunate death of President Kennedy, however, again raised the specter of doubt concerning the *Alianza* by removing the one person who had inspired faith in it.

The San José Conference

President Francisco Orlich of Costa Rica considered every possible security precaution to protect the lives of six other American heads of government and one president-elect who were scheduled to meet in San José on March 18, 1963. The nations participating in that conference cooperated by sending large retinues of bodyguards who took up positions of vigil throughout the capital city of Costa Rica. At times the precautionary steps bordered upon the ridiculous; some reporters complained, for example, that they were unable to enter the building where they were supposed to get their working credentials. Yet, in fairness to Costa Rica, it should be noted that she could not afford to relax her efforts in the face of rumors that an attempt would be made on the life of President Luis Somoza, the scion of a Nicaraguan dynasty that was highly unpopular among the *Ticos* of Costa Rica. Somoza, at any rate, did not consider the rumors baseless. Seventy agents guarded his every move, and his place of residence during the San José Conference was a well-guarded secret.[2]

[2] Special report, Paul P. Kennedy, New York *Times* (Western Ed.), March 18, 1963.

On the day before President Kennedy's arrival United States officials discussed the agenda of the three-day conference with the chief executives and foreign ministers of Panama and the five Central American countries, making it clear to them that their government would not allow the meetings of the next few days to serve as a forum for the discussion of its policy toward Cuba. Since the missile confrontation of October 1962, and because of its world-wide implications, the Kennedy administration had to insist upon sole responsibility for that policy. Although disappointed by this restriction, the chief executives agreed that Cuba would not figure directly on the agenda; the San José Conference would focus attention instead on the Alliance for Progress and the economic integration of Central America and Panama.

Miguel Ydígoras of Guatemala and Luis Somoza of Nicaragua were particularly annoyed at the decision to avoid any discussion of Cuban policy, an understandable feeling in view of their governments' unqualified commitment to the forceful overthrow of Fidel Castro. The ill-fated expeditionary force to Cuba, after all, had been trained in Guatemala and had embarked from Nicaragua. At Punta del Este in Uruguay later in that same year the two countries unreservedly supported a strong policy toward Castroism in the Western Hemisphere, and several weeks before the missile confrontation they participated in the war games at Tegucigalpa, maneuvers which brought anxious moments to the Communist satellite in the Caribbean. To be sure, Panama and other Central American countries had also demonstrated a willingness to contain *Fidelismo*, but not to the same extent as Guatemala and Nicaragua. It was no coincidence, therefore, that Cuban subversion should focus upon them; conversely, the instinct of survival compelled Ydígoras and Somoza to push their Northern ally to a commitment to the forceful overthrow of Fidel Castro.

If the Kennedy administration did not want to air its Cuban policy, what then did it hope to accomplish by the San José meeting? Certainly it was not necessary to discuss the *Alianza* or the Central American common market at the presidential level; others had done this already.

The answer would appear to lie in the American political scene.

Hailed for his energetic stand on the missile question, JFK soon found his popularity slipping as the impression gained credence that a *modus vivendi* had been arranged with the Russians. His critics were demanding nothing less than the complete withdrawal of Russia's personnel from Cuba. In this context, the San José Conference becomes meaningful: it could distract attention from the pesky Cuban question and at the same time permit President Kennedy to educate his people on the merits of the *Alianza*—his long-range solution to the threat of communism in the Western Hemisphere. And Costa Rica was an ideal showcase for dramatizing the possibilities of this approach.

The San José Conference might serve other objectives as well by helping to convince all Latin Americans that the United States sincerely wished to assist them in realizing their dream of a higher standard of living and a more democratic society. At those meetings, moreover, JFK would have an excellent opportunity to address his Central American allies, some of whom reportedly were supplying the administration's critics with "facts" and "attitudes" to the effect that all Latin Americans favored the forceful ouster of Fidel Castro, regardless of the risks. He could remind them of their responsibility for implementing the *Alianza*'s reforms and show them that force and undemocratic means were not the only solution—if they were any solution at all—to the threat of Castroism. The educational task confronting President Kennedy at San José was indeed a formidable one.

On Monday morning, March 18, a tumultuous reception greeted the American President as a quarter of a million Costa Ricans poured over the four-mile stretch from the airport to downtown San José. The good-natured crowd made a shambles of its government's elaborate security measures; demonstrating their nationalism, *Ticos* surrounded the procession's lead car occupied by Orlich and his distinguished guest. Other chief executives and dignitaries had no choice but to lag behind, some twenty minutes late. Costa Rica had welcomed JFK with an open heart, and he was deeply moved.

That afternoon, at the National Theater, President Kennedy delivered his "wall-around-Cuba" speech, announcing to the world that there had been no appeasement of Russia since the missile crisis and that the Alliance for Progress was not the unmitigated failure that some commentators were claiming, certainly not in Central America. "With the help of dedicated and brave men," he prophesied, "we will ultimately triumph over aggressors of today." And though Cuba was under the despotic will of the Soviets, Americans would not permit any further expansion of communism. He added with emphasis: "At the Organization of American States, at this meeting, and wherever Americans gather to consult about the future of their continent, we will continue to strengthen the structure of resistance to subversion." Turning to the common market theme, the President congratulated Central Americans on their efforts to integrate their economies, a laudable project which the United States would continue to support because it held the promise of a higher standard of living and a more balanced economy for Central America. "To this end," he added, "we must push forward plans for industrialization, greater crop diversification, strong educational facilities and better utilization of resources." [3]

President Julio A. Rivera of El Salvador, as chairman of the first afternoon session, likewise keynoted the major objectives of the conference. He spoke of the unionist ideal in Central America—the enduring desire of Guatemalans, Salvadoreans, Hondurans, Nicaraguans, and Costa Ricans to form a single republic, just as they had done in the early nineteenth century upon achieving independence from Spain. The economic union of the five Central American sisters, in addition to their Panamanian neighbor, might well prepare the ground for realizing the political dream. He urged the various delegations therefore to accept unanimously those measures which would help to implement the common market project and the institutional reforms of the *Alianza para el Progreso*.[4] President Rivera's words left no doubt that here at least was one ally committed to the long-term policy of the Kennedy administration. And this was not mere oratory; El Salvador had already gone far beyond token gestures of reform.

Despite the earlier agreement, certain Latin presidents could not refrain from bringing up the Cuban issue. President Kennedy found

[3] As quoted in the *Arizona Daily Star* (Tucson), March 19, 1963.
[4] Special report, Paul P. Kennedy, New York *Times* (Western Ed.), March 20, 1963.

it necessary to spend nearly three hours on the morning of the 19th briefing his allies on United States-Russian relations since October, explanations that fell upon the deaf ears of at least one president, who argued recklessly that Moscow was bluffing and that an invasion of Cuba would involve no risk. But Kennedy held his ground. As the leader of a powerful nation with world-wide commitments and responsibilities, he could not be stampeded into an action which might harm the real interests of his country in Latin America and the world over just to satisfy the personal frustrations and objectives of a Central American chief of state. And there the matter rested. The teacher had made his point.

The "Declaration of Central America," signed on Tuesday afternoon, was a brief and vague document which dealt mainly with economic matters. According to its terms, the United States offered to provide $6 million for a regional survey which would determine how much money would be needed to establish the common market and when it should be allocated. Although not explicitly stated, it was generally understood that American financial support would be in the neighborhood of $200 million. The Declaration contained the usual statements favoring institutional reforms, and the signatories agreed to combat Cuban subversion by various means, including restrictions on the movement of nationals to that island. In short, the San José Conference seemed to have produced tangible results.

As a matter of fact, the main fare of the meetings was President Kennedy's speechmaking and extracurricular activities. To the despair of the Secret Service, JFK mixed freely among the denizens of San José, who lionized their *Pepe Bueno* (Good Joe) and followed him everywhere. On Tuesday afternoon he dramatized the achievements of the *Alianza* by visiting the housing project at El Bosque, scheduled to be completed in October 1963, and by examining mobile hospital units of the type which eventually would provide four million medical examinations annually throughout Central America. In a "symbolic token of a massive program which will introduce more than 2,000,000 new primary school textbooks into Central America and Panama," he presented books to six children from the Middle American area. Extolling the *Alianza para el Progreso*, and reminding his audience of the common nineteenth-century struggle for liberty in the Americas, President Kennedy recalled what Franklin Delano Roosevelt had said in 1936 at Buenos Aires: "Through democratic processes we can strive to achieve for the Americas the highest possible living standards for all our people." [5] Sensing the magic of his predecessor's name in Costa Rica and throughout Latin America, he again evoked FDR's memory on the following day with these famous words: "I can say here to you: This generation of Americans —your generation of Americans—has a rendezvous with destiny." [6]

These were sheer strokes of genius. Costa Ricans went wild, shouting themselves hoarse with *vivas* for Kennedy, their new Good Neighbor. In his final speech JFK reciprocated with "*Viva Costa Rica, muchas gracias.*" Sweeping down all barriers, his *Tico* friends escorted him to his plane. It was one of the most enthusiastic farewells that the lanky American leader had ever received; certainly, it was sincere.

Back in Washington on Thursday evening, President Kennedy reported to his nation at six o'clock, rather than at four, in order to reach a larger audience. He spoke optimistically about the *Alianza* and how it was succeeding in Central America, at the same time giving the impression that his administration's policy toward Cuba was responsible and well conceived. But members of the press were not especially cooperative. From the beginning of the interview they kept asking him specific questions about Cuba: how many Soviets had been withdrawn, and so forth in the same vein. In his answers the President continued to bring up the Alliance for Progress and the significance of the recent talks in San José.[7] His audience apparently did not get the point.

Even if President Kennedy had lived, historians of the future undoubtedly would have marked the San José Conference of March 1963 as a milestone in his policy toward Latin America, a sincere and determined attempt to breathe reality into the *Alianza* and thus to

[5] Text of John F. Kennedy's speech, San José, March 19, 1963, in the New York *Times* (Western Ed.), March 20, 1963.

[6] As quoted in the *Arizona Daily Star* (Tucson), March 21, 1963.

[7] The New York *Times* (Western Ed.), March 25, 1963, contains an excellent synthesis of the San José Conference in "The News of the Week in Review" section. Tad Szulc's evaluation and observations in the March 19 and 20 issues were especially useful in writing this section.

recapture the heart and imagination of Latin America for the cause of the free world. His tragic death gives the San José meetings even more historical significance: it was his last personal move to redirect his country's Latin American foreign policy, in contrast to what his successors may do to a program that reflects his genius. Unfortunately, since his death the spirit of the Alliance for Progress, at least as he envisioned it, has been changed, if not distorted, by the military dictatorships which have plagued Latin America. Two of Kennedy's Central American allies have fallen by the wayside since the San José Conference.

To determine the validity of President Kennedy's approach to Central American affairs, let us now consider the physical realities of the area—its geography, ethnography, social structure, and economy —and what they portend for the vaunted common market. Then, we shall examine the political realities, so essential in appreciating what possibilities exist in implementing the institutional reforms outlined in the Alliance for Progress. Finally, we shall look at the special relationship of Panama to the Central American complex, stressing the impact of the United States-Panama crisis of early 1964 on the whole region.

Physical Realities

The five countries of Central America offer a variety of geographical features in a territory that encompasses nearly 180,000 square miles. The most conspicuous topographical feature is a rugged mountainous terrain, edged by extensive coastal lowlands on the Pacific and Caribbean flanks. The highest points of elevation are in the peripheral states of Guatemala and Costa Rica, and though the mountain systems are lower in the center states, they are nonetheless imposing obstacles to effective communication. Except for Nicaraguans, the bulk of Central America's 11 million people (a 1960 estimate) live at high altitudes on intermountain plateaus (*mesetas*) where the climate is temperate, an important consideration in the tropics. Of the national capitals only Managua falls below the 2,000-foot line; in fact, most Nicaraguans dwell in the Pacific lowlands and along the narrow structural depression which traverses the country diagonally from the Gulf of Fonseca in the northwest to the Caribbean

Sea in the southeast, following the line formed by Lake Managua, Lake Nicaragua, and the San Juan River.

The ubiquitous dust which loaded the atmosphere at the San José meetings brings to mind one of the area's major characteristics—its volcanic activity. Just prior to the opening of the conference one member of the quartet of volcanoes guarding the northeastern approach to San José—the famous Irazú—again spewed forth its smoky innards. The last time this happened, in 1910, Irazú almost leveled Cartago. The number of *Ticos* suffering respiratory diseases has reached alarming proportions, livestock has been destroyed, and agriculture has suffered tremendous losses. Some Costa Ricans are even thinking about moving their capital city to avoid Irazú's wrath, not an uncommon historical occurrence in Central America. There are at least 21 active volcanoes throughout Central America, not to mention the numerous cones that are dormant. Over the centuries volcanic eruptions and the earthquakes associated with them have taken a heavy toll of lives and property; none of the Central American countries has escaped these periodic misfortunes. On the positive side, volcanic ash has enriched the soil—though human and climatic factors have tended to reverse the process—and volcanoes have added to the majestic beauty of Central America, a veritable paradise for tourists. In recent years the common market planners have initiated steps to develop the tourist trade, a potential of no mean consideration.

The harsh terrain of Central America has made communication from one population center to another difficult. Transportation systems have always been poor, inadequate, and expensive because there have not been enough people along a given route to justify a more efficient network of roads and railroads. To be sure, the countries are now linked by an elaborate air service and the Inter-American Highway, but the common market needs more than this. From the historian's viewpoint, the lack of adequate transportation and communication facilities helps to explain the exaggerated sense of localism that has worked against the effective union of Central America.

As might be expected in highland zones located in the tropics, there is considerable diversity of climate and vegetation depending upon the elevation and the position of a given locale vis-à-vis the moisture-bearing winds. On the Caribbean coast there are lowlands and tropical forest extending inland as much as 50 miles. This is the *tierra caliente*, a hot and humid area with excessive rainfall that leaches the soil of important ingredients. It was here that the banana industry flourished during the early decades of this century until the *sigatoka* and Panama disease forced the gradual transfer of banana plantations to the lowlands on the Pacific coast. With the application of modern techniques banana plantations have reappeared in the Caribbean zone. Incidentally, the most extensive lowland area does not front on the Caribbean; it is the Department of El Petén in Guatemala, west of British Honduras, a limestone tableland and tropical forest which ranges from 500 to 700 feet in elevation. For many years this empty land was visited only by chicle gatherers and curious scholars investigating the famous ruins of the Mayas. With the recent discovery of petroleum deposits there has been more activity in the area and the population has increased. Some agricultural communities have been established there under Guatemala's agrarian program.

In the interior, with increasing elevation comes a dramatic change in climate and vegetation. Semideciduous trees appear, the rainfall is adequate, and coffee plantations thrive in what is called the *tierra templada*, the temperate zone on the slopes and plateaux of the highlands, where most Central Americans live. At the highest elevations the *tierra fría* (cold zone) is characteristic. Water is often a problem, especially on the leeward side of the eastern escarpment that blocks the water-bearing winds from the north and east. In the highlands the rainy season is from May to October, the so-called *invierno* (winter) because of the inclement weather and relative lack of sunshine by comparison with the rest of the year. In some localities the moisture is sufficient for one annual crop; in other places arid wastes and the type of vegetation associated with them add to the complex topographical mosaic.

In contrast to the gentle Caribbean slopes, the descent from the highlands to the Pacific is abrupt, the lowlands extend only from 10 to 25 miles in depth, and the weather is hot and arid except during the rainy season from May to October. Along the slopes of the highlands coffee and banana plantations are profitable enterprises. Water is a serious problem in the Pacific lowlands. At some times the rainfall is meager; on other occasions there are floods caused by torrential downpours and by the resulting cascades of water from the highlands. Here, as elsewhere in Central America, erosion is a problem—the result of nature's fickleness and man's wasteful practices. The flooding and silting, moreover, have limited the use of harbors on the Pacific coast with the exception of the ports in the Gulf of Fonseca, shared by El Salvador, Honduras, and Nicaragua, which have facilities for large ships. On the Caribbean the ports are adequate for normal coastal traffic; the need here is for better transportation links with the hinterland.

Judging from the facts brought out in the foregoing discussion, the economic integration of Central America will not be easy. The basic facilities will be expensive, much more than Central Americans will be able to afford in the immediate future. They will need financial support from the outside, both private capital and government loans. In addition, Central Americans must be prepared to invest in their own future and to plan their projects carefully. Certainly they can no longer postpone drastic conservation measures to prevent further erosion and excessive deforestation of the land. In short, they must reckon with the physical realities of their area.

But Central America's disunity and problems cannot be attributed solely to physical obstacles; equally responsible are the lack of ethnological and cultural homogeneity and the societal pattern that has dominated the area since the Conquest. No matter which demographic studies we consult or what criteria have been used in compiling statistics, the fact is evident that ethnic diversity has always existed in Central America. In Guatemala, for example, the descendants of the Mayas are the dominant racial and cultural element, dwelling for the most part in the western and southern highlands. Constituting roughly two thirds of the population, these Indians live in isolated communities which in turn display a wide range of cultural differences. Another 30 per cent of Guatemala's inhabitants is *mestizo*, a mixture of Indian and white with the former predominating. The whites account for only about 3 per cent, and the Negroes, less than 1 per cent. Ethnically Guatemala is an Indian country, yet the real social leaders are white. At the other end of Central America, in Costa Rica, the ratios are almost reversed. Whites and *mestizos*, in whom white rather than Indian predominates, form 95 per cent of the population; Negroes make up 3 per cent of the total, and Indians, only 2 per cent.

In the center states the *mestizo* is the dominant type. If we add the number of Indians to the number of mixed bloods—this combination is valid since there is no cultural differences between them, as there is in Guatemala—the average is 87 per cent. Whites range from 5 per cent to 10 per cent; Negroes, from 5 per cent to 9 per cent.

As for population density and growth, according to 1961 estimates Salvadoreans are pressing upon the land at the rate of 125 persons per square kilometer; Guatemala is next with 35.4, followed by Costa Rica's 23.2. The two empty countries of Honduras and Nicaragua have 16.9 and 10.2 respectively. These figures suggest that Central America, except for El Salvador, is underpopulated. Yet account must be taken of the area's population explosion; the percentages would be much higher if better sanitation prevailed and infant mortality were not so great. As it is, all five countries show an annual rate of increase ot at least 3 per cent. The exact figures for 1961 are as follows: Costa Rica, 4 per cent; El Salvador, 3.5 per cent; Nicaragua, 3.4 per cent; Honduras, 3.3 per cent; and Guatemala, 3 per cent.[8]

This is all the more remarkable considering the low standard of living of most Central Americans. The majority exist at subsistence level. Only one third of the people are members of the area's work force and thus constitute the potential consumers for common market products. With a limited purchasing power of $2.5 billion annually, the projected economic complex does not look promising. According to 1960 estimates the per capita income for the various countries is as follows: Costa Rica, $406; El Salvador, $195; Honduras, $192; Nicaragua, $183; and Guatemala, $163. The area's average is $208, or one third that of the United States. By comparison, Puerto Ricans averaged $587 in 1960; Central America is now at the same level Puerto Rico was in the early 1940s.[9]

[8] Julian S. Duncan, "Demographic Factors and Economic Integration in Central America," *Journal of Inter-American Studies*, Vol. V, No. 4 (October 1963), 542.
[9] Frank L. Keller, "ODECA: Common Market Experiment in an Under-Developed Area," *Journal of Inter-American Studies*, Vol. V, No. 2 (April 1963), 267-75; Joseph Pincus, *El mercado común centroamericano* (Mexico City, 1963), p. 8.

The nucleus of potential consumers for the common market lies principally in El Salvador and fans out to the southern portion of Guatemala, to the western and northern districts of Honduras, and the northern and western portions of Nicaragua. By utilizing the natural facilities of the Gulf of Fonseca and by improving the network of roads into Honduras the common market will have a substantial base upon which to build—providing the purchasing power of Central Americans can be increased. Costa Rica and Panama are accessible by both water and land, now that the Inter-American Highway has been completed. A boon to the common market would be the construction of the vaunted interoceanic canal between Nicaragua and Costa Rica to link the Caribbean ports to the above-mentioned complex. Needless to say, Panama, as an associate member, would not welcome such an innovation.

Historically, racial diversity and cultural differences have had a disruptive effect upon Central America. At present, tensions arising from these divergencies are less acute thanks to the widespread process of "ladinoization." During the colonial period Spanish overlords used the term *ladino* in reference to Indians who had adopted the white man's way of life and worked as artisans in Spanish towns. They were Indians who had been "Latinized," so to speak. Over the years the term also came to be applied to mixed bloods—*mestizos*, mulattoes, and *zambos* (Indian and Negro)—who gathered around white settlements. The current official meaning of *ladino* is any person, regardless of racial ancestry, who does not live like an Indian. Used in this sense, the term has positive implications for a Central American nationalism by binding together discordant racial and cultural elements. But this bond was not present in Central America's past; on the contrary, discrimination was a source of tension and explosiveness to that society. Moreover, it would be foolish to assume that it is absent in the contemporary scene. Many upper-class whites in Guatemala, for example, refuse to call themselves *ladinos* because they consider the term equal to *mestizo*.

In the last analysis, racial and cultural differences are negative factors only because of the type of society that was established after the Conquest. White minorities seized control of the land and resources and thus became undisputed leaders of the government, the economy, and the society of their respective regions. They are the old established "families" of Central America today, often referred to as the "decent people," "the aristocracy," and so forth. Within their ranks there are recognized strata; generally, the older the family, the higher its rank in this class-conscious society. Professor Richard Adams refers to the top element as "cosmopolites," a highly cultured and sophisticated set that lives in the national capital rather than on the family estate and has contacts with the leading families of the world. Below them is the "local upper class," whose members reside on their estates or in provincial capitals; their family trees also have deep roots. Recently a new wealthy element has been recognized, one based on business and speculative agriculture.[10] In all cases the elite groups are one in keeping the lower classes in their place by all forms of discrimination, some not so subtle. In their range of values the more Indian a person happens to be the less civilized he is considered. Their inferiors are viewed as scamps—shiftless, dishonest, treacherous, and even biologically inferior. The white elite therefore takes great pains to separate itself from the masses by obeying certain customs, living in special neighborhoods, and belonging to exclusive clubs. At one time they even insisted upon different burial grounds. Accustomed to centuries of dominion, they will insist upon maintaining it at all costs. A dictatorship has been the standard device in the past.

The majority of Central Americans have ample grounds to resent the overwhelming power of the masters, or *patrones*. They live in depressed conditions and at the mercy of the white landowner who determines how many workers he needs and what he will pay them. In fact, the point has been made frequently that Central America's competitive position in the world coffee market is due to the labor surplus that this type of society fosters.

A sizable middle class has been closing the gap between the very rich and the very poor in Central America since the latter part of the nineteenth century. Once a mere sliver in the societal pyramid,

[10] Richard N. Adams, "Social Change in Guatemala and U.S. Policy," in *Social Change in Latin America Today* (Council on Foreign Relations: New York, 1960), pp. 242-47. For a more detailed analysis see his *Cultural Surveys of Panama-Nicaragua-Guatemala-El Salvador-Honduras* (Washington, D.C., 1957).

the middle classes now comprise large numbers of intellectuals, professionals, artisans, small farmers, bureaucrats, and persons from the
lower echelons of the Church and army. To these traditional middle-
class elements have been added new groups created by the increased
tempo of the economy and greater contacts with the outside world:
office workers, skilled labor, business experts, teachers of all levels,
and so forth.

These modern middle sectors have been demanding a greater
political voice and tend to be more nationalistic than the upper
classes. In Costa Rica, for example, they generally favor a more democratic way of life and the modernization of their nation's economy
and society. In other countries, where their desires have been frustrated, they have been fully able and willing to support dictatorships
of the Left. That was the case in Guatemala. Yet many members of
this middle group aspire only to identify themselves with the traditional upper classes and therefore willingly support dictatorships of
the Right in order to maintain law and order.

The Central American common market will also have to overcome
the weaknesses of monoculture and the competitive nature of the
individual economies. In the past Central Americans have geared their
energies to the production of goods for outside markets; 95 per cent
of their output, for example, has been shipped regularly to the United
States, Canada, Japan, and Western Europe. This unduly heavy dependence upon outside markets means that they are vulnerable to
price fluctuations, over which they have no control, in the world
market and to competition from other sources of supply—coffee from
Africa, bananas from Ecuador, only to cite a few cases. An annual
balance of payments deficit is customary in their trade relationships
with the more advanced industrial nations.

How is the common market expected to improve upon this situation? Since all the countries produce just about the same products,
there is little future in exchanging bananas, coffee, and cotton among
themselves. By united action, however, they can hope to improve
their chances of influencing world prices for those commodities. But
their bargaining power is limited; they simply are not that important
as suppliers of those products in the international market. Rather, the
future of Central America's common market lies in promoting a

greater diversification of export products and in developing the industrial potential of the area.

Moreover, the Central American countries have tended to emphasize
the same processing industries and the same competitive domestic
industries that provide the local market with shoes, clothes, tobacco,
and sundry items. In developing a regional market there will have to
be agreement on the division of labor. This will not be a simple
matter, for vested interests in each country will certainly make emotional appeals to their respective governments. Despite these obstacles, many industries have already been "integrated"—that is, they
have been given a monopoly of the regional market. Political considerations figure strongly in the distribution of those industries; each
country expects the same treatment and guards against favoritism to
others. The political approach is working now because there are
many new industries yet to be founded. At a more advanced stage
of economic development and planning the rivalry undoubtedly will
be keener.[11]

The program to develop the present common market of Central
America dates back to mid-1950 and was strongly influenced by the
world-wide movement to form regional organizations and by the
perennial dream of Central American union. On October 8, 1951, the
foreign ministers of the five countries met in San Salvador to discuss
the feasibility of organizing on a regional basis. There were those
who favored the restoration of the Central American Republic which
expired in 1839. But others, perhaps more realistic in view of the
failures that plagued the union movement in Central America, preferred a nonpolitical integration that would place the emphasis upon
forms and projects of unified action that had a reasonable chance of
success. These in turn might pave the way for eventual political
union. On October 14, 1951, the delegates signed the Charter of San
Salvador which established ODECA (*Organización de Estados Centro*

---

[11] In late 1961 the Committee for Economic Cooperation indicated at least
11 possible fields of endeavor which the common market nations were urged to
consider. They were (1) refined petroleum, (2) fertilizers, (3) insecticides and
fungicides, (4) veterinarian, biological, and pharmaceutical items, (5) tires and
tubes, (6) paints, varnishes, and dyes, (7) ceramic products and glass, plastic,
and metal containers, (8) fish, (9) soldered tubing, (10) absorbent cotton, and
(11) woods, pulp, and paper. See Pincus, *op. cit.*, p. 40.

Americanos), a body charged with developing policies and advancing the objectives of union. Approved by the member states, ODECA began its official existence on December 14, 1951.

ODECA's formative years—that is, until June, 1958—set important precedents for the future in a political context that threatened to undermine its constructive labors. When Guatemala learned that the Salvadorean State Department was planning to present an anti-Communist resolution at the first biennial meeting of foreign ministers, Colonel Jacobo Arbenz withdrew his country from ODECA. That was on April 4, 1953. Guatemala returned to the fold in mid-1954, soon after Colonel Carlos Castillo Armas took over the government. The Costa Rican-Nicaraguan armed encounter of early 1955 and the tension between El Salvador and Nicaragua arising from the assassination of Anastasio Somoza in 1956 further embarrassed the efforts toward union; so too did the spirited competition between Costa Rica and Guatemala over the appointment of the second secretary-general of ODECA in 1959. Fortunately, a compromise was reached in February 1960 with the election of the Costa Rican Marco Tulio Zeledón.[12] This crisis, so typical of the historic jealousies of the Central American states, nearly wrecked ODECA.

In the nonpolitical realm the progress toward union was impressive, as illustrated by the numerous and enthusiastic meetings of lawyers, educators, students, economists, and others. Recognizing the need for public administrators and trained technicians, Central American leaders sanctioned two key educational institutions: one, the *Escuela Superior de Administración Pública para la América Central*, established in 1954 in San José, Costa Rica, to train public officials; the second, the *Instituto Centro Americano de Investigación y Tecnología*, founded in Guatemala City two years later. And thanks to the close cooperation of the United Nation's ECLA (Economic Commission for Latin America), basic surveys and studies of Central America's economy and resources were conducted and resulted in a series of recommendations by the participating experts.

Perhaps one of the most successful ventures in nonpolitical cooperation has been the Institute of Nutrition of Central America and

[12] James L. Busey, "Central American Union: The Latest Attempt," *The Western Political Quarterly*, Vol. XIV, No. 1 (March 1961), 49-63.

Panama (INCAP), which opened its doors two years before ODECA was organized. Under the capable leadership of Dr. Nevin S. Scrimshaw, presently at the Massachusetts Institute of Technology, INCAP has trained many Central Americans in the field of nutrition while at the same time conducting basic research on the nutritional patterns and needs of the people. INCAP's progress has been dramatic, and Scrimshaw's successors—Drs. Moisés Béhar, Ricardo Bressani, and Guillermo Arroyave—continued the good work, expanding the province of INCAP's training to include doctors and nutritionists from other countries of the Western Hemisphere. The product *Incaparina* has been the object of considerable publicity because of its effectiveness in helping to eliminate protein malnutrition and the diseases associated with it. Specialists in other parts of the world are striving to duplicate this food supplement which, being made of indigenous products, is reasonably priced and culturally acceptable to the lower classes of Central America and Panama. INCAP's success speaks more authoritatively for the benefits of union than thousands of banquet speeches and reams of paper on the subject.

From June 1958 to December 13, 1960, the governments of Central America signed no less than eight trade agreements which implemented the recommendations of economists. The present common market, the *Mercado Común Centroamericano* (referred to as the *Mercomún*, or MCC), derives from the General Treaty of Central American Economic Integration, signed in Managua on December 13, 1960, which went into effect on June 3, 1961, upon being ratified by Guatemala, El Salvador, and Nicaragua. Honduras and Costa Rica had affixed their signatures to the document by November 1962. Some products already have "national" character and can circulate freely in the regional market; others will be added to the free list during the six-year transition period, thus avoiding any drastic dislocations in local economies. By June 3, 1966, the common market should be fully operative. In due time there will be a common nomenclature for goods, a standard tariff, a uniform system of taxes and controls, and mobility of labor and capital within the region. The General Treaty also favors the development of industry and the establishment of regional credit institutions such as the Bank of Central American Economic Integration in Tegucigalpa, Honduras.

Three major organs are responsible for carrying out the General Treaty: first, the Executive Council, consisting of one delegate and one alternate for each country, which implements resolutions by majority vote; second, the Central American Economic Council, made up of the economic ministers for all five states, which is responsible for directing the integration process; and third, the Permanent Secretariat (SIECA: *Secretaría Permanente del Tratado General de Integración Económica Centroamericana*), located in Guatemala City, with a secretary-general appointed for a three-year term by the Economic Council. Older bodies supplement the new organs of the General Treaty; ODECA, in San Salvador, now concentrates on political integration and social development, including health and education.

The *Mercado Común Centroamericano* has progressed satisfactorily since the San José Conference despite the political pressures and considerations which inevitably arise. Having the highest purchasing power, and being by tradition isolationist, Costa Rica has been reluctant to open up her domestic market to products from her sister states where labor costs are less. Honduras tends to frown upon the intrusion of Salvadorean families into her territory, while El Salvador, on the other hand, is anxious to relieve the population pressure upon her limited resources. Perhaps these bones of contention will disappear once the benefits of economic union become visible.

Financial support for the economic complex seems adequate so far. In establishing new banking institutions the countries have faithfully contributed their proportional shares, and the United States government and special agencies like AID (Agency for International Development) have provided key loans. Moreover, private capital, both foreign and domestic, appears willing to back the "integrated" industries of Central America. So long as the emphasis of union remains economic, the prospects for the *Mercomún* are encouraging. But it will be a slow process, one fraught with obstacles, and its social and political implications may not be realized for decades.

Political Realities (1954-1965)

Central America has been experiencing a "revolution of rising expectations" since World War II. A major objective of that "revolution" has been the democratization of political institutions, a goal that Central America, with the exception of Costa Rica, has only partially and haltingly been able to realize. Since the Costa Rican experience vindicates the *Alianza's* democratic emphasis, we shall evaluate her political history in this section in order to contrast it with developments elsewhere in Central America during the past decade. In a later chapter we shall treat the more violent expression of the 1944 "Revolution" in Guatemala.

COSTA RICA

Before 1948 the political power structure in Costa Rica differed only slightly from that of her northern neighbors. Since more people owned land, and the middle class was therefore larger, popular representation had been established as early as 1889. Yet personalist politics, so typical of "traditional" Latin America, was still very much in evidence. The ideological content of politics was scanty; elections were nothing more than periodic contests between rival political bosses and their minions. Real control of the government rested in the hands of large landowners and foreign corporations, and the electoral process was characterized by nepotism, corruption, and spoils. Although 20 per cent of the population was eligible to vote, very few actually bothered to exercise this right. Most *Ticos* had no political voice; they spent their lives in poverty. The economy of Costa Rica was colonial in nature: food production was inadequate, the dependence upon imports further depressed the living standard of most Costa Ricans, and foreigners had practical control of business, banking, and commercial agriculture.

The depression of the 1930s was a turning point in Costa Rican history, for it caused thinking people to question the old order and to study the problems of their national existence. Some turned to Communism for solutions, and the Communist party of Costa Rica, founded in 1929 by Manuel Mora, began to participate actively in domestic politics, influencing much of the welfare legislation which appeared in the depression years. In the process, the political system began to change somewhat; it seemed to be accommodating itself to the times.

The more liberal elements in society, however, were not satisfied with the degree or the nature of this political change, and they gathered in study groups which eventually entered the political arena as the *Acción Democrática* and later as the *Partido Social Demócrata*. In contrast to the old parties, this new political force had a pronounced ideological content, advocating a democratic political structure, social reforms, and a revamping of the national economy—a program which appealed to the middle sectors, labor, and well-to-do businessmen.

During World War II these reformers challenged the administration of Dr. Rafael Angel Calderón Guardia (1940-44). Drawing his support from professional politicians, rich landowners, and Communists who were capitalizing on Russia's alliance with the democracies, President Calderón backed the candidacy of Teodoro Picado, a prominent lawyer, in the elections of 1944. The *Calderonistas* won the election by the use of fraud; the opposition reacted violently, but to no avail. The defeat increased the reformers' determination to rid the country of *Calderonismo*. The climax was reached in 1948 when Calderón stood for re-election and the reformers gathered behind Otilio Ulate, the well-known editor of the *Diario de Costa Rica* and a conservative in political outlook. Ulate won the election, but the legislature, packed with *Calderonistas*, found a flimsy pretext for annulling the results on March 1, 1948. Costa Rica thus fell into civil war.[13]

During the months of fighting which ensued both sides received substantial outside support. The dictators of Nicaragua (Anastacio Somoza) and Honduras (Tiburcio Carías Andino) aided the Picado-Calderón-Communist coalition, while President Juan José Arévalo of Guatemala helped the revolutionary forces under José "Pepe" Figueres. Ironically, the *Calderonistas* later cited this alliance as proof of Figueres' Communistic tendencies—a clear-cut case of the pot calling the kettle black. When the rebels emerged victorious, a provisional junta was established. On May 8, 1948, Figueres was named head of this junta with the understanding that after 18 months he would relinquish power to Otilio Ulate, the lawful victor of the 1948 elections.

[13] Professor Harry Kantor has two excellent studies on the subject of this discussion. See his article "También hay democracia en el Caribe," *Combate*, No. 9 (Marzo y Abril 1960), 56-67, and his monograph, *The Costa Rican Election of 1953: A Case Study* (Gainesville, 1958).

During its incumbency the *Junta Fundadora de la Segunda República* (Founding Junta of the Second Republic) put into effect a series of basic reforms that have since become solidly institutionalized. Some of the junta's acts and reforms were drastic and even vindictive, reflecting years of frustration and anger toward the pillars of the old regime. For example, the junta dissolved the Costa Rican army, leaving only a police force to maintain order; it banned the Communist party; and it levied a capital tax that fell most heavily upon the rich, a revenue that presumably would help pay for the damages incurred during the recent hostilities. The junta also nationalized the banking system and paved the way for a civil service organization to end the baneful practices of the *personalista* era. The new constitution of 1949 gave women the suffrage, modernized education, and provided for social welfare. This was no mere barracks coup; a revolution had taken place.

The bold strokes of the revolutionary junta did not go unchallenged. From Nicaragua as a base, and with the support and blessings of "Tacho" Somoza, a small expeditionary force of *Calderonistas* invaded Costa Rica—a standard practice in Central American history. The expedition failed miserably, as did a subsequent invasion in 1955 from the same base and by the same parties. The victory increased the popularity of the provisional government. On April 2, 1949, an armed coup was also quashed in short order. The revolution had succeeded. As promised, Figueres turned over the reins of government to Ulate on November 8, 1949, establishing a precedent that has been faithfully observed since then and that has given Costa Rica her world-wide democratic image.

During the Ulate administration (1949-53) Costa Rica enjoyed peace and prosperity, thus stabilizing the financial foundation of the Second Republic. High prices for coffee and other exports netted valuable revenue, and the nation's credit standing was enhanced by a settlement with the United States Bondholders' Council. Thus, loans were made available for an extensive public works program that further stimulated the economy. By ignoring the junta's 10 per cent capital levy and replacing it with an export tax on coffee, Ulate endeared himself to businessmen and further encouraged the wave of prosperity. In late 1951 he announced a two-year development program to increase agricultural and industrial productivity and at the same time to stimulate the diversification of agriculture. The Point Four program contributed to this effort with its valuable experimentation at Turrialba, some 30 miles east of San José.

Despite impressive progress in material and fiscal matters President Ulate, as a conservative, chose not to advance forcefully in the realm of social reforms, thus losing the support of the Figueres elements. In 1952 "Pepe" Figueres helped form the PLN (*Partido Liberación Nacional*) to reach the Costa Rican masses with a platform dedicated to the achievement of effective democratic institutions and the abolition of poverty. He campaigned vigorously on this platform in the electoral campaign of 1953 and won the elections handily. José Figueres, a wealthy coffee planter and entrepreneur, once again headed the government, this time as the elected choice of his compatriots.

Like the New Deal in the United States, the Figueres administration still arouses controversy. His enemies, whose cooperation with the Communist party is a matter of record, do not wince at calling the diminutive leader a Communist for the socialistic measures the PLN has introduced—the nationalization of banks, of insurance companies, of utilities, and so forth. Apparently they choose to overlook his consistent and militant stand against the Costa Rican Communist party and his vigorous anti-Castro policy. There is no love wasted between Fidel Castro and the PLN, that is certain. The opposition has also accused Figueres of demagoguery, maintaining that he established autonomous state organs for urban housing, tourism, social security, and civil service just to reward his followers with governmental positions. His tariff of 1954, intended to nourish infant industry, has been described as ruinous to the economy and a serious imposition upon local consumers.[14] All of his enemies persist in blaming him for the economic crisis of 1958, blandly overlooking the recession in the United States that brought a drop in coffee prices.

However valid these charges and accusations may be—certainly, they must be qualified and their motivations understood—we should try to understand the philosophy which has guided the PLN and similar parties throughout Latin America. In the long run they may

[14] John D. Martz, *Central America—The Crisis and the Challenge* (Chapel Hill, 1959), pp. 249-50.

prove to be the best allies of the United States. To begin with, the movement headed by José Figueres is highly nationalistic, one which sincerely and fervently aspires to improve and modernize Costa Rican life, economy, and government along more democratic lines. By and large, the manifestations of this nationalism have been positive rather than negative.

Figueres and his followers believe in a mixed system of economic enterprise in which public and private capital collaborate for the good of the nation's inhabitants. Their approach is above all pragmatic and experimental, not doctrinaire. In some aspects their program is socialistic, pure and simple; in others it is what might be called constructive liberalism, an approach which has an historical precedent in Central America. During the early nineteenth century many liberals throughout the world believed that government had positive responsibilities toward members of the body politic—to provide education, make internal improvements, and implement all measures which would help responsible individuals to develop the economic potential of the nation. In the twentieth-century context, however, constructive liberals no longer stress the virtues of competition and the evils of monopoly; they believe that bigness and the monopoly which attends it are not necessarily bad, providing that the government can regulate the process and prevent abuses from taking place.

The sensible and realistic arrangement of June 4, 1954, between Figueres' government and the United Fruit Company (UFCO) illustrates the pragmatic nature of this type of constructive liberal and what foreign investors can reasonably expect from him as long as they are willing to accommodate themselves to the nationalistic aspirations of his nation. In the campaign of 1953 Figueres averred that he would not tolerate foreign investors who expected special concessions not enjoyed by nationals and who ignored Costa Rica's juridical sovereignty by making direct appeals to their home governments—another stand with a long historical precedent in Central America. On the other hand, he promised unlimited support to foreign capitalists who shared his faith in Costa Rica's future and were willing to abide by the nation's rules. In modern Costa Rica the government would eliminate the risks which had served as justification for earlier concessions; it would guarantee law and order and assume responsibility for all the requisite social services. He insisted that UFCO would have to pay one half of its profits to the Costa Rican government rather than the 15 per cent income tax of the former contract, and that it could no longer enjoy special exchange rates and duty-free imports.

As it turned out, the new contract represented a compromise. UFCO agreed to pay 35 per cent of its net earnings in addition to some minor taxes, bringing the total to 42 per cent. The company promised, moreover, to pay custom duties on about half of its imported materials; supplies for needed improvements on railways, harbors, drainage controls, and so forth would continue to come in free of duty. UFCO likewise subscribed to the government's minimum wage decree. In return, Costa Rica assumed financial responsibility for the company's schools, hospitals, and recreational facilities. In short, the 1954 contract, which is binding for 34 years, permits UFCO to continue making profits without offending national pride.[15] And it should be noted that the Figueres government opposed the antitrust action against the fruit company in the United States, arguing that its size and methods of operation led to more good than bad.

The Figueres presidency was a constructive period in Costa Rica's history. National revenues increased, thanks to a continuation of high prices for Costa Rican commodities; public works modernized the faces of towns and cities; new roads were completed, including the Inter-American Highway to Nicaragua; electrical power facilities were doubled; pastoral industries flourished to the point that Costa Rica became an exporter of meat; and agricultural experiment stations encouraged higher productivity. The moral fervor of the revolution extended to the implementation of laws against alcoholism and prostitution, much to the annoyance of the vested interests concerned.

Despite the PLN's popularity, and because of a division in its ranks, the conservatives' candidate won the 1958 elections by a scant 6,000 votes, though the legislature remained under the PLN's control. The wealthy business element in the party, unwilling to support any more experimentation and reform, defected to the conservatives and provided the margin of victory. Throughout the presidency of Mario

[15] *Ibid.*, pp. 246-48.

Echandi from 1959 to 1962, primarily because of the legislature's hostility to him—he was enthusiastically hooted down whenever he spoke before it—Costa Rica witnessed four years of drift in govern-ment.[16] The revolution now advanced at a slower pace, but it is significant that it did continue under Echandi's presidential guidance. During his tenure Costa Rica joined the *Mercomún* and contracts were issued to enterprises that were to participate in the regional market, further industrialization was encouraged by various incentives, additional foreign power interests were liquidated, and the petroleum industry was stimulated. In September 1961 Costa Rica severed relations with Castro's Cuba. These were all actions that had the PLN's wholehearted support; otherwise, they never would have passed.

Having mended its political fences, the PLN had little trouble in winning the 1962 elections. Under President Francisco Orlich the "Revolution" is going through a phase of consolidation. In foreign affairs Orlich is an outspoken enemy of Fidel Castro; in July 1964 he urged the OAS to impose sanctions on Cuba for having introduced arms into Venezuela. Although a firm ally of the United States, the Orlich government does not hesitate to criticize its neighbor's policy, especially the recognition of military regimes that have ousted demo-cratic Central American governments since the San José Conference. When the New York *Times* reported in early March 1964 that the State Department might abandon its policy of withholding recogni-tion and *Alianza* funds from *de facto* governments, the *Ticos* were not at all pleased. Until August 1964 Costa Rica, for example, refused to recognize Peralta's Guatemala; but it seems to have reconsidered its former policy because of the effect that it might have on the *Mercomún*. Also, a Costa Rican rubber concern, backed by Firestone, is eager to share the regional tire and tube market with the "inte-grated" Guatemalan company, Ginsa.

GUATEMALA

Since 1954 Guatemalan governments have been contending with the legacy of the revolutionary decade of Juan José Arévalo and Jacobo Arbenz. Despite the rightist inclinations of her leaders,

[16] James L. Busey, *Notes on Costa Rican Democracy* (Boulder, 1962), p. 42

Guatemala has actually consolidated and forwarded the materialistic objectives of the 1944 "Revolution," thanks to aid from the United States. The spirit and orientation of these reforms, however, are noticeably different.

In a recent book by Miguel Ydígoras Fuentes, *My War with Communism*, the ex-President of Guatemala maintains that while living in exile in El Salvador he was visited by a former executive of UFCO and two gentlemen introduced to him as agents of the C.I.A. Hoping to capitalize on General Ydígoras' popularity among Guatemalans, they had come to discuss with him the possibility of leading an armed expedition against Arbenz. When he asked them bluntly what conditions he would be expected to meet in the event of victory, they told him that he had "to favor the United Fruit Company and the International Railways of Central America; to destroy the railroad workers' labor union; to suspend claims against Great Britain for the Belize territory; to establish a strong-arm government, on the style of Ubico," and to pay back a loan which would cover the expedition's expenses.[17] Ydígoras refused the terms, and his visitors left. The implication is that subsequently Carlos Castillo Armas had no such scruples.

At a later date Castillo Armas also interviewed Ydígoras in San Salvador. During the course of their conversation the young Colonel told him "that he had the promise of assistance from official United States agencies, an offer from the Government of Honduras to give him asylum and allow the common border with Guatemala to be used for the attack, that the Government of Nicaragua had also offered him arms and bases for training troops, and that Generalissimo Rafael Trujillo of Santo Domingo was generously supplying him with substantial economic assistance and large quantities of arms." [18] Upon receiving Castillo Armas' promise that free elections would follow the downfall of Arbenz, Ydígoras gave his blessings to the expedition and signed a "gentlemen's pact."

Whether by coincidence or intent, the Castillo Armas tenure in Guatemala from 1954 to 1957 conformed to the terms which Ydígoras

[17] Miguel Ydígoras Fuentes, *My War with Communism* (Prentice-Hall, 1963), p. 50.
[18] *Ibid.*, pp. 50-51.

had been asked to meet by his American visitors. He ruled like a Jorge Ubico, the Guatemalan dictator who had fallen from power in 1944; his version of "free elections" in October 1954 was nothing more than a dictator's plebiscite—only oral votes were counted. Ydígoras broke with Castillo Armas because of this. A secret National Defense Committee Against Communism, using crude gestapo-like methods, stifled all opposition to Castillo Armas. Anyone who had supported Arbenz, for whatever the reason, was automatically suspect, and the prisons overflowed. Only the lack of facilities and the added expense of caring for political prisoners finally cooled the ardor of the NDCAC. This unnecessary and indiscriminate persecution of non-Communists—the real Communists had long since left the country—deprived Castillo Armas of an important source of trained personnel who had supported Arbenz for nationalistic reasons.[19] In contrast to the Arévalo-Arbenz era, the press was muzzled by the Law of Public Order, and in 1956 the new constitution gave the president authority to withhold civil rights in cases involving the security of the state. This was indeed an Ubico-type government.

Labor suffered a setback during those years because the NDCAC pointed an accusing finger at practically all labor leaders. Whereas in 1954 there were some 330 unions with a membership of 107,000, a year later the number dropped to 27 with a mere 27,000 members. Labor leaders—those allowed to operate—clamored for the abolition of the NDCAC, classifying it as a union-breaking device that served the interests of the United Fruit Company and the Association of Guatemalan Agriculturalists. But their protests fell on deaf ears. Finally, in May 1957 labor leaders threatened to withdraw support from the government if it persisted with its antilabor measures. It was undoubtedly pressure from the Regional Inter-American Workers Organization that forced the dictator to comply. In mid-1957 he accepted such measures as the minimum wage law and the right of agricultural workers to form unions.

Large landowners and foreign corporations whose lands had been confiscated by Arbenz received favorable treatment from the new government, which immediately revoked the Agrarian Law of 1952.

[19] Nathan L. Whetten, *Guatemala—The Land and the People* (New Haven, 1961), p. 342.

Lands were returned to their former owners, and the government moved the recent settlers to other plots, though the problem of squatters was never adequately solved. New agrarian legislation in February 1956 permitted the expropriation of lands, especially those that were not being exploited, under conditions of payment more equitable to the owner, and the proprietors of new homesteads received titles in perpetuity rather than on a lifetime basis as formerly. The emphasis of Castillo Armas' agrarian program was on resettlement. The government conscientiously strove to improve communications to newly opened areas, to provide the requisite technical education, and to select the right type of colonists. From the scientific viewpoint, the new program was a decided improvement over the old. The advantage, it would seem, stemmed from the financial support of the United States and the know-how of its experts. Yet critics of the program maintain that it was too limited in scope and that it did not meet the needs of Guatemala's agricultural community.

Guatemala's economic development was impressive by any standards during the three years that Castillo Armas ruled his country. As in the case of Costa Rica, the prosperity resulted from high prices in the world market for Guatemalan commodities. In addition, the United States government and its various agencies plowed some $90 million into the economy. The Castillo Armas regime planned its economic actions carefully, utilizing the Institute for the Development of Production (INFOP: *Instituto de Fomento de la Producción*), which Arévalo had set up in 1948. In November 1954 it outlined a five-year development program whose objectives were the diversification of Guatemala's economy, the increase of light and power facilities, the expansion of agricultural productivity, and greater efficiency in governmental procedures. Private enterprise, both foreign and domestic, would help achieve those goals.

The constitution of 1956 was avowedly submissive to foreign capital, and Castillo Armas' treatment of foreign interests stood in marked contrast to that of his predecessors. Relations with UFCO were almost idyllic, the company forsaking some of its expropriated lands for grants elsewhere in Guatemala. In its new contract, which is to run until 1981, the company agreed to pay 30 per cent of its profits to the government. Other American firms, especially oil companies, were generously encouraged by favorable legislation such as the Petroleum Code of August 9, 1955. And by the end of the decade oil had been struck. Investors from the United States were also active in establishing industries scheduled to participate in the Central American common market—the tire and tube industry is a case in point. Needless to say, the antilaborism of the Castillo Armas government proved to be a key incentive for the industrial surge of those three years.

In economic terms the Castillo Armas administration represented a step forward, made possible by the financial support of the United States. An embryonic Alliance for Progress—without the democratic requirements, to be sure—had been forged in the crucible of Guatemalan politics. Yet we must not forget that much of Guatemala's economic progress was made at the expense of the nation's labor movement, of the nationalistic policies of previous administrations, of civil liberties, and of democratic institutions in general. The United States' identification with, and open support of, Castillo Armas' regime, moreover, had significant hemispheric repercussions in arousing suspicions throughout Latin America concerning the United States' intentions and position vis-à-vis the "revolution of rising expectations" in those countries. *Fidelismo* and Latin America's reluctance to follow the United States' lead against Castro are attitudes of mind that were nourished by the Guatemalan events just described.

The strong arm of Carlos Castillo Armas was felled by the trigger finger of a palace guard on July 27, 1957. After hectic months of interim governments in which factions struggled for position, Miguel Ydígoras, a 60-year-old General who had served Ubico and was identified with the conservatives of his country, was elected to the presidency. He assumed power on March 2, 1958.

Despite President Ydígoras' efforts to disassociate himself from the government of his predecessor, the past weighed on him relentlessly. During the first year of his rule the economic advance in agriculture and industry continued as outlined by Castillo Armas. New industries were added—a paper mill, a flour company, and others. In a bid for popularity with labor Ydígoras nationalized the Guatemalan railways in January 1959 and gave raises to the workers. But the economic spurt was short-lived; a drop in coffee prices led to deficits in the National Treasury, followed by a curtailment of governmental programs and the initiation of austerity measures which caused ripples in the political waters.

Although he had desperately hoped to win the plaudits of his countrymen, President Ydígoras found himself in a delicate political position, unable to please any substantial sector of the population. The Left did not trust him; as far as they were concerned, he was another Castillo Armas, a mere tool of the oligarchs and foreign interests. And the Right felt that the General's reforms, and the middle position he occupied on most questions, would lead Guatemala to another violent revolution. To divert attention from domestic problems Ydígoras challenged Great Britain on the Belize Question, reasserting Guatemala's long-standing claim to so-called British Honduras. But even this was not enough to offset the growing unpopularity of his administration, now beset by recurring rumors and disclosures of fraud and corruption. When the opposition became too vociferous, the volatile General lost his head and resorted to those clauses in the constitution of 1956 that permitted him to rule dictatorially, thus forsaking his almost pathetic concern for democratic procedures. Guatemala's frustrated President could not cope with the forces of discontent generated during Castillo Armas' regime.

When the dust settles and the historian is able to view the Ydígoras years dispassionately, he will probably record that the General's popularity waned because he offended the nationalistic spirit of his countrymen—a seemingly far-fetched verdict in the light of Ydígoras' sincere patriotism. But there are many ways to express one's nationalism, and Ydígoras apparently chose the wrong way to express his. For whatever the reason—and it seems that Ydígoras, like his military brethren throughout Latin America, was obsessed with the dangers of Communism and Castroism—he chose to cooperate with the C.I.A. in bringing down Fidel Castro by force. By early 1960 there were already rumors that Guatemala was helping to outfit and train an expeditionary force of Cuban exiles. From that time forward the Ydígoras administration was under constant pressure by leftists and moderates who regarded the General's actions as antinationalistic and the General himself as a mere tool of the United States. At this time Castro was still considered a respectable revolutionary; he had not yet declared himself a Communist.

Guatemala and Cuba broke diplomatic relations in late April 1960 after an acrimonious exchange of words and notes. The Guatemalan Left kept up its harassment, and Ydígoras reacted with a state of martial law that lasted from July 19 to October 12. Significantly, during a parade honoring the October 1944 "Revolution" participants stoned the American Embassy. From November 15 to 17 an abortive army coup took place, which Ydígoras blamed on Communists and Castroites. It was on that occasion that President Dwight D. Eisenhower sent naval units to the Caribbean coasts of Middle America without consulting the OAS. In Guatemala, Eisenhower's action was interpreted as an attempt to bolster the puppet Ydígoras. And finally, after many denials, the not-too-well-kept secret was announced to the Guatemalan people: Ydígoras admitted that Cuban exiles were being trained at Retalhuleu.

After the Bay of Pigs invasion in April 1961, students clashed with members of the National Defense Committee Against Communism in the streets of Guatemala City, provoking Ydígoras to call another state of martial law. The popularity of leftist parties surged accordingly, and Guatemalans flocked to the ranks of the *Partido Revolucionario* (PR), headed by Mario Méndez Montenegro. Even formei President Juan José Arévalo's name was bandied about in political circles as a possibility for the next presidential elections. In August 1962 an extremist splinter group broke away from the PR; this was the *Partido Revolucionario Ortodoxo* (PRO), which terrified the Right and brought anxious moments to the man in the Presidential Palace. The PRO favored Arévalo's candidacy in no uncertain terms on a platform which included: (1) true agrarian reform, (2) a speed-up in industrialization, (3) support of trade unionism, (4) religious and political freedom, (5) an independent position in foreign affairs, (6) rejection of foreign ideologies, and (7) Central American economic integration. On November 26 Arévalo announced his candidacy from Venezuela and publicly disclaimed any sympathy for Fidel Castro. In short, the ill-fated Cuban invasion had brought the Left back into favor, and it had an attractive presidential candidate running on a platform that was completely acceptable under the Alliance for Progress.

President Ydígoras, in the meantime, tried to counter the Left's challenge by encouraging a series of reforms called for in the *Alianza*, but the nation balked, especially at the introduction of the income tax. With the economy still in the doldrums, the time could not have been less propitious; "traditional" Guatemala had not lost her aversion to taxes, and the Left was determined to discredit the administration. The old General's popularity hit rock bottom on November 26, 1962—the day Arévalo announced his candidacy—when the air force staged a revolt, a rightist coup of officers closely associated with the slain Castillo Armas. The Right wanted no income tax and was especially alarmed at the prospects of another term for Arévalo—the pesky October 1944 "Revolution" was on their doorsteps again, as if nothing had happened in the interim. In February 1963 a special anti-Arévalo committee threatened the ex-President if he dared return to Guatemala by holding him accountable for the mysterious death of Colonel Francisco Arana in 1949 and insisting that he be brought to trial for that dastardly crime.

Ydígoras shared the apprehensions of the Right, and on returning from the San José Conference he revealed his hand. He announced on March 21, 1963, that he had in his possession Arévalo's Communist party card number. The ex-President was therefore, said Ydígoras, not eligible to re-enter the country—a decision which the Supreme Court overruled on the 22nd, declaring Arévalo eligible for re-election. Ydígoras held his ground, while the Right paraded through the streets of Guatemala City in protest. University students and groups favorable to Arévalo put on counterdemonstrations, and two guerrilla bands in the north rebelled against the government—all of which prompted another proclamation of martial law on March 25, less than a week after Ydígoras bade farewell to JFK.

A display of force overwhelmed the Guatemalan Left. At Ydígoras' request his ally Somoza dispatched three jets to Guatemala City. The "pro-Castro" revolt had to be put down at all costs; even Ambassador John O. Bell of the United States felt that Arévalo was a Communist, unfit for the presidency of Guatemala.

The ouster of President Miguel Ydígoras remains clouded in mystery. Allowed to cross the Mexican border, Juan José Arévalo appeared briefly in Guatemala City on March 31. This, in turn, served as the pretext for compelling Ydígoras to give up his office, a maneuver directed by Colonel Enrique Peralta Azurdia, Minister of Defense. In Managua, on the first step of his exile, Ydígoras made this now classic observation: "What is going on in Guatemala is for its own good and for the good of the rest of Central America." Later, in Miami, the ex-President denied rumors that he had anything to do with Peralta's coup, and since then he has maintained an official position of opposing Guatemala's military regime. Peralta likewise has stubbornly refused to countenance any meddling by Ydígoras.

Undoubtedly, the Peralta coup represents the determination of the military, supported by rightists, to prevent the take-over of the government by the liberal and nationalistic Left. It is not likely that the United States government had anything to do with the coup, Ambassador Bell's indiscreet remarks notwithstanding. Discredited by the Cuban debacle, it is also reasonable to assume that the C.I.A. was not involved. A more plausible explanation is that it was an exclusively Guatemalan affair in which the military acted on its own, taking its cue from similar military actions in South America and presenting the United States with a *fait accompli*. Peralta gambled—and here it is conceivable that private American interests in Guatemala may have encouraged the move—that the Kennedy administration would have no choice but to recognize the new government, especially in view of the United States' obsession with Castro. And the gamble paid off. Shortly after President Kennedy's assassination the Johnson government recognized the Peralta regime and restored *Alianza* funds solely on the promise that constitutional government was forthcoming.

After 15 months of decree-law government, during which political parties of the Left were purged and defanged, Colonel Peralta felt reasonably satisfied that it was safe to give constitutionalism another try. Perhaps he had little choice in the matter if he expected further aid from the United States. At any rate, on July 6, 1964, the National Constituent Assembly opened its sessions. Politicians of the Right dominate this body, and it is reasonably certain that they will constitutionalize the acts of the Peralta government. They will do this not only to please the military power but also because the decree-laws protect and conserve the prerogatives of the upper classes in Guatemalan society. Mario Méndez Montenegro, despite opposition within his *Partido Revolucionario*, has decided to participate in the proceedings of the Assembly in order to preserve the Left's voice in the government. It remains to be seen how effective he will be.

In the meantime an aura of constitutionalism prevails in Guatemala City, as newspapers discuss the relative merits of certain reforms and decree-laws. Occasionally a spokesman for the government has to bring them down to face reality—the naked military force that rules Guatemala and that is frequently displayed in ceremonies and parades, as if to awe the citizenry. *Prensa Libre*, fighting for the freedom of the press, received a not-too-subtle reprimand from the government in the early days of July.[20]

THE CENTER

The overthrow of Arbenz in Guatemala in 1954 vitally affected political developments in nearby Honduras, where Castillo Armas launched his revolutionary enterprise. After years of inaction because of the long dictatorship of Tiburcio Carías Andino, the Liberal party capitalized upon Honduran nationalistic sentiment, which opposed President Juan Manuel Gálvez' support of Castillo Armas, to win the elections of 1954. Ramón Villeda Morales was their standard-bearer. The narrow margin of victory for Villeda, however, served as the excuse for a political shake-up in which, though Gálvez was deposed, the Liberal party was denied its prize and Vice-President Juan Lozano took over the government. This elderly gentleman ruled dictatorially for the next two years. When it appeared that he planned to make the arrangement permanent, a group of young officers pronounced against him on October 20, 1956, and prepared the nation for elections. Villeda Morales was again the victor; he began his six-year term on December 21, 1957.

In both ideological outlook and approach the new President had much in common with José Figueres of Costa Rica. Though his accomplishments were not as dramatic as his neighbor's, they were nonetheless impressive by Honduran standards and in view of the

[20] *Prensa Libre* (Guatemala City), July 3, 6, 7, 1964.

power of the conservatives. During his administration Honduran economic development advanced noticeably, partly a result of general world prosperity, partly because of government action and *Alianza* support. The educational system was modernized and expanded, and democratic institutions matured to the point that an effective two-party system appeared to be in the offing. In the political conventions of early 1963 the conservatives and liberals deliberately selected compromise candidates: the Liberal party nominated the moderate Luis Modesto Rodas Alvarado, relegating the choice of the far Left to one of the vice-presidencies, and the National party chose a respectable judge, Ramón E. Cruz, instead of Carías Andino's son or Colonel Oswaldo López Arellano of the militant Right. But on October 3, 1963, just two and one-half months shy of completing his full term, Villeda Morales succumbed to the military power of López Arellano, who emulated Peralta's example in Guatemala.

Elected on a platform of nationalism and liberal reforms, Villeda Morales maintained cordial relations with the United States, though he avoided any impression of dependence on or subservience to that Northern republic. He demonstrated his independence, for example, by favoring nonintervention in Cuba and by refusing to cooperate in a Cuban invasion. A week after the Bay of Pigs episode, nevertheless, Honduras broke off diplomatic relations with Cuba and has backed a hard line against Castro ever since. From the Honduran viewpoint, Villeda Morales acted wisely in not supporting the Cuban expedition. Aware of the nationalistic views of both the Left and Right, he could not have done otherwise without exposing himself to the same troubles Ydígoras and other Central American leaders faced during the critical years of 1960-61. After all, his party had gained a new lease on political life by criticizing the Gálvez regime for its involvement in Arbenz' ouster.

The Agrarian Law of September 1962 illustrated the nationalistic pressures under which a democratically elected president had to operate in Honduras. Progressive in nature, the law underscored the social responsibility of private capital and called for an enlightened program of agrarian reform. Since abundant lands for such a purpose were available, this was one requirement of the Alliance for Progress that Honduras found easy to meet. Yet the Agrarian Law contained a section which prohibited foreigners from living or owning land within 30 miles of the seacoast, a security precaution not uncommon to other nations of the world. American fruit companies, as might be expected, immediately protested that the implementation of that section would harm their economic interests along the Honduran coast. When Villeda Morales fell from power, the issue was still alive; it remains to be seen what the López Arellano regime will decide to do about this matter. If it supports the fruit companies, some observers will undoubtedly cite this as proof that American interests were behind the recent coup.

As in Peralta's case, President Johnson recognized the López Arellano government when it promised to hold general elections by 1965. Although recognition of those two *de facto* governments was inevitable and necessary, the same cannot be said for the decision to supply them with *Alianza* funds which made a sham of the program's democratic postulates.

During the last decade El Salvador's impressive material accomplishments have proceeded under the direction of progressive military leaders. As far as democratic institutions are concerned, however, the record is less encouraging: Salvadoreans have a choice only between rival military factions whose political instruments dominate the electoral process by various means. Traditional societal patterns, in the meantime, have not been unduly disturbed. El Salvador's revolution has been of the gradualist variety, one that the nation's aristocracy has condoned in order to prevent any drastic change in its way of life.

From 1944 to 1949 El Salvador went through a transition period in which various military figures tried to inherit the mantle of the old *caudillo*, General Maximiliano Hernández Martínez. Major Oscar Osorio emerged victorious from the scramble. In March 1950 he began a six-year term as president backed by a party of his own creation, the *Partido Revolucionario de Unificación Demócrata* (PRUD), which controlled Salvadorean politics in the fifties.

The PRUD administrations of Osorio and his hand-picked successor, José María Lemus (1956-60), brought the modern world to El Salvador. Using scientific methods, the government embarked upon an ambitious program to revamp and diversify the economy. An important agency in bringing this about was the Salvadorean Institute for the Development of Production (INSAFOP: *Instituto Salvadoreño de Fomento de la Producción*), founded in 1955, which conducted studies and formulated plans to stimulate the nation's economic life. As a result, new agricultural exports lessened dependence upon coffee as an exchange-getter in the world market; the fishing industry and light industrial enterprises helped to balance the economy and to provide work for El Salvador's burgeoning population; housing and highway construction further improved the nation's welfare; tourism was encouraged on a large scale for the first time; and the Lempa River's electrical potential was harnessed by dams and power plants, making El Salvador the recognized Central American leader in this field. High coffee prices made the development program possible. Although social security, public health, and the improvement of rural living conditions were governmental objectives, they were not implemented to any great extent, nor did real agrarian reform go beyond the paper stage. The military leaders preferred not to antagonize the country's elite.

President Osorio pursued an independent policy of opposition to the Communist threat. Fearing the presence of Communists in his country, perhaps linked to those of Guatemala, he declared martial law in 1952 and subsequently banned all subversives from participation in politics. The following year El Salvador asked the Organization of American States to investigate Communist activities in Central America, a request which led to Guatemala's resignation from ODECA. Yet he refused to back the Castillo Armas expedition, reasoning that the Arbenz government was unstable and would not last long in power. Nonintervention further stabilized Osorio's regime.

PRUD's record in domestic politics, however, undermined its popularity, contributing to the party's eclipse in 1960. Determined to stay in office, Osorio's partisans resorted to every cheap political trick in the book to thwart their rivals. In this way the party alienated key military and civilian figures—for example, Roberto E. Canesa, a prominent civilian who had served briefly as Minister of Foreign Affairs under Osorio—who might have helped PRUD stay in power. The rigged presidential elections of 1956 in behalf of José María Lemus proved to be the last straw. While prosperity continued, the

Lemus government had been tolerated, but a drop in coffee prices and the attendant financial problems put the opposition in an ugly mood that was intensified by PRUD's heavy-handed politics in the legislative elections of 1958 and 1960. In 1959 even Osorio broke with Lemus, forming the PRUD *Auténtico*. When Lemus chose to confer with President Miguel Ydígoras in early October 1960, giving the impression that El Salvador was also supporting the Cuban exiles, his days in office were numbered.

A junta of six army officers overthrew the Lemus government on October 26, 1960. Initially it seemed that the new regime expressed the will of all Salvadoreans against the tyrant, but as the weeks passed, it became abundantly clear that the junta represented an ultranationalistic viewpoint sympathetic to Castro. The United States withheld recognition until December 3. In the meantime, fearing confiscation of their property, foreign investors began to liquidate their holdings and fled the country, compounding the financial troubles of the provisional government.

Within three months there took place a counterrevolution that was anti-Communist and anti-PRUD. Its leaders blamed both Osorio and Lemus for the leftist orientation of the previous junta. The new directorate, which consisted of three civilians and two military men, assumed power on January 24, 1961; from its ranks emerged the present incumbent of El Salvador, Colonel Julio Adalberto Rivera. Closely identified with the United States, the new government maintained order during the critical year 1961 and held elections in 1962, at which time Rivera began his five-year presidency.

Although civilians are prominent in the present government of El Salvador, its orientation is predominantly military. Political democracy exists in theory only. There are encouraging indications, however, that this progressive military regime—and it should not be classified along with those of Guatemala and Honduras—is preparing the nation for free political institutions by conscientiously fulfilling the requisites of the *Alianza para el Progreso*. It is continuing not only the impressive developmental program of the PRUD administrations but also the social reforms that they had neglected. The regime has the support of the labor movement, and management and labor are displaying a remarkable spirit of compromise which augurs well for El Salvador. Rural workers are receiving tangible benefits for the first time, though they still are not permitted to form unions.

The administration's major problem—indeed, a formidable obstacle confronting the *Alianza*—is to convince the Salvadorean aristocracy, and the middle classes as well, that effective social and fiscal reforms can no longer be delayed. The alternative is a Castro-type revolution that will destroy them. Representatives from the United States are working closely with the Rivera government to bring this basic point home.

El Salvador is second only to Costa Rica in reaching the standards set by the *Alianza*, displacing from that position the Honduran experiment that was left truncated by the military coup of October 1963. In contrast to Costa Rica, however, El Salvador will have to contend with a serious psychological obstacle—its people's sensitivity to any intimate connection with the United States. And this obstacle, a very real one from the Salvadorean viewpoint, cannot be taken lightly. The United States must cope with this historical factor realistically rather than emotionally if it hopes to advance its real interests throughout Latin America. From exile and from underground, extreme leftists and ultranationalists are bombarding the Salvadorean populace with propaganda that Rivera has sold out to the greedy imperialists and the "neo-colonialist designs" of the *Alianza para el Progreso*. To combat this propaganda effectively and thus permit our allies to save face among their own people, we must prove our sincerity and good intentions in supporting and furthering the original objectives of the *Alianza*. If we relegate the Alliance for Progress to the status of an oratorical device and make its money available to groups that do not share its democratic objectives, it will be a sheer waste of time and resources on our part. More than military force is needed to combat the enemy in Latin America; the battle for man's mind is even more important in the long run, even though it is exasperatingly slow and seemingly unrewarding at times. President Kennedy understood this lesson well; it should not be forgotten by his countrymen.

Voltaire's famous dictum, "The more things change, the more they are the same," aptly characterizes Nicaraguan history since the assassination of Anastacio Somoza on September 21, 1956. It is still

"Somozaland" in every respect. Anastacio Jr. ("Tachito") controls the powerful national guard just as his father did for years, and Luis, the heir apparent, experienced no difficulty in winning a six-year term as president, from 1957 to 1963. The economic development of Nicaragua has been more rapid and extensive than in other Central American countries, but the Somozas and their closest friends are still the principal beneficiaries of the projects that are undertaken. Labor organizations abound, but the national guard watches them closely so that they will not take themselves too seriously. Somoza's Liberal party tolerates "liberalism" only in theory; press censorship is standard procedure, the constitution and presidential oratory notwithstanding. The constitution grants minority representation, but this concession applies only to conservatives, *Zancudos*, who play the game according to Somoza rules. Respectable and legitimate conservatives like Pedro Joaquín Chamorro Cardenal, editor of *La Prensa*, refuse to dignify the farcical elections with their participation and are constantly persecuted by the government when they are not in exile. Chamorro's pen—interestingly, the Somozas cannot silence him for long because of his world-wide renown—has scathingly exposed the hypocrisy of his nation's institutions. Independent liberals also chafe under the Somoza yoke.

With the blessings of the Somozas, René Schick Gutiérrez was permitted to win the elections of early 1963, the first secret ballot contest in Nicaragua's history. Promising to continue his predecessor's policy of free speech and freedom of the press, President Schick also reaffirmed his nation's commitment to a forceful stand against Fidel Castro. So far the Schick government has been an improvement over the past administration, though it would be difficult indeed to convince union men and student demonstrators of this. One thing is certain: Mr. Schick will not be allowed to stray far from the path. The national guard will see to this.

Yankeephobia is a permanent state of mind among the Somozas' opponents, regardless of their ideology. The historical and close attachment of the United States with Father Somoza—it was not until 1961 that Ambassador Thomas Whelan, a card-playing colleague and advisor of the old dictator, was recalled—helps to explain this antipathy. Furthermore, Luis Somoza cooperated with the C.I.A. in the

Cuban venture, receiving in turn valuable military aid that helped keep the lid on the domestic pot. In the first five years of Luis Somoza's term there were four years of martial law, which demonstrates the strength of Nicaraguan sentiment against cooperation with the United States. And the military aid from the Northern republic continues to the present. In April 1962 the Somoza government purchased four jet planes in the United States—some of which were used to frighten the Guatemalan Left, it will be recalled. In the meantime Nicaragua has been deemed to meet the requirements of the *Alianza para el Progreso*, at least to the satisfaction of the proper authorities in Washington.

The Panamanian Neighbor

Historically Panama is not a Central American country, though she has much in common with her neighbors to the north, especially with the three center states. Sixty-five per cent of her people is *mestizo*. A white minority controls politics, society, and the economic life of the nation. Transportation facilities are poor and inadequate, and the economy is underdeveloped and monocultural. Her relationship with the United States has always been close. During the 1950s, moreover, Panama frequently sent observers to ODECA meetings, and on occasion she invited Central American experts to carry on their discussions in Panama City. At the San José Conference President Roberto F. Chiari pleased his Central American colleagues with the announcement that Panama might be willing to join the Central American common market as an associate member, thus adding another million consumers to the regional market. Despite these promising indications, it is doubtful that Panama will actively join Central America's integration program until it is a going concern. Her links with Colombia and South America, as well as her special relationship with the United States, will probably delay her participation in the *Mercomún* for many years to come.

The Panama Canal crisis of January 9-10, 1964, received extensive coverage in Central America's newspapers, as it did throughout Latin America, and the overwhelming sympathy of the public was behind the underdog, Panama. But while the press justified the Panamanian reaction and students demonstrated in Nicaragua and Costa Rica, the various governments of Central America officially refrained from taking sides. The Peralta regime in Guatemala was especially careful not to antagonize the United States lest it be cut off from *Alianza* funds. There was governmental reaction, however, to talk of constructing a new canal through Nicaragua—an old dream that has fascinated man since the Spanish Conquest. The Costa Rican government hinted that it desired a review of the Bryan-Chamorro Treaty of 1914 (ratified by the United States Senate in 1916). That unpopular treaty, which will be discussed at greater length in Chapter Three, gave the United States the right to construct a canal through Nicaragua and to maintain a base on the Gulf of Fonseca. Other Central American nations now insist that Nicaragua had no right to give concessions that affected their own sovereignty. Costa Rica has complained that the proposed canal route follows much of her northern border, and the nations sharing the Gulf of Fonseca likewise feel that a U.S. base in Nicaragua jeopardizes the freedom of their commercial activities in that area. Central America, in short, wants no part of the Bryan-Chamorro Treaty because of the historical example of the Panama Canal. If a canal is to be constructed through Nicaragua, the arrangement will have to be made on another basis. Like Mexico, Central America will probably insist upon her sovereign rights to such a passageway.

Although this is not the place to discuss the recent Panama Canal crisis in detail, we can profit by examining the historical and psychological factors that help to explain why Central Americans, and Latin Americans in general, sympathized with Panama.

The United States actively encouraged the Panamanian revolt that brought independence from Colombia in 1903, a fact well known to historians. In an embarrassingly short time the Northern power recognized the new nation, concluding with it the Hay-Bunau Varilla Treaty. This document gave the United States jurisdictional rights to a strip of land ten miles wide that traversed Panama in a north-south direction—that is, the "rights, power, and authority" that it "would possess and exercise if it were the sovereign." In no way did this concession impair the "titular" sovereignty of Panama, according to the interpretation of Latin American jurists and international lawyers in general. United States Secretary of War William Howard

Taft first made this point clear in 1906 and with the approval of President Theodore Roosevelt.

The treaty notwithstanding, the United States actually restricted Panama's sovereignty over all of her territory from 1903 to 1939 by insisting on the United States' right of intervention in Panamanian domestic affairs. According to Washington the security of the Canal Zone, which was opened to interoceanic traffic in 1914, justified this right. Panamanians, of course, resented the United States' attitude and especially the peremptory refusal of their guardian to meet their frequent requests for changes in the 1903 treaty. Not until 1936, when the United States went off the gold standard, was the annual rent raised from $250,000 to $430,000. Three years later the United States formally gave up its right of intervention.

During World War II, Panama made available to the United States additional territory for air bases and radar stations in return for money payments. When the war was over, the State Department rather carelessly ignored the stipulation in the agreement of 1942 whereby the United States had agreed to evacuate the installations within a year after the signing of a peace treaty. A dangerous emotional situation arose when the United States failed to meet the September 1, 1946, deadline. The following year nationalistic fires burned white as the State Department, determined to get a renewal of the bases agreement, went over the Foreign Minister's head to the President of Panama. The net result of this high-handed action, so typical of the pre-1939 period, was the unanimous defeat of the renewal treaty by the Panamanian Legislature and the evacuation of the bases.

José Antonio Remón was the strong man of Panama from 1947 to January 1955, when an assassin's bullet brought him down. Having started as chief of police, he was elected to the presidency in 1952. During his few years in office he ruled much the same as Osorio did in El Salvador, taking giant steps to modernize the economy of his country. He was especially intent on renegotiating the Canal treaty of 1903.

These were the grievances that Remón's negotiators presented to the United States government: First, Panama felt that the annual rent arrived at in 1936 was inadequate, especially since Canal tolls amounted to over $37 million a year and since her revenues from that land before the construction of the Canal had been higher than the rent paid. Second, Panamanian businessmen resented the unfair competition of commissaries in the Canal Zone, which consistently undersold them and took away their customers. At one time, they argued, the existence of commissaries was understandable, but this was no longer the case. And finally, Panamanians objected to the discrimination practiced by Canal Zone authorities—the segregation of local people into separate schools and housing, and different pay schedules. Whereas 5,000 whites from the United States received the "U.S. rate," colored Panamanians and mulattoes, whose ancestors had helped to build the Canal, got the "local rate." [21]

Realizing that these grievances merited a hearing, the Eisenhower administration agreed to participate in negotiations. These dragged on for 16 months; finally, in March 1955, a new treaty was signed and subsequently ratified. It reflected a commendable effort to reach a suitable compromise. In return for a higher annual rent of $1,930,000, Panama made available 20,000 acres for training and military maneuvers around the important air base of Río Hato on a 15-year lease, rent free, and the United States promised that it would first consult Panama before using those lands. The 1955 pact restricted U.S. importation privileges in the Canal Zone, reduced the competition from Zonian enterprises and abandoned some of them, and most importantly, incorporated for the first time the concept of a basic wage scale for all employees.

The Egyptian seizure of the Suez Canal on July 26, 1956, complicated matters once again. The American Secretary of State, John Foster Dulles, infuriated Panamanians when he prevailed on Great Britain to exclude Panama from the 22-nation conference in London, hoping thus to discourage her from imitating Nasser's example. And on September 28, 1956, he compounded the injury by maintaining that Panama had no sovereign rights to the Canal Zone. Shortly thereafter, Canal authorities initiated a single wage plan under which employees recruited in the United States received a 25 per cent dif-

[21] Martz, *op. cit.*, pp. 282-93, is excellent on this subject.

ferential and local workers got the U.S. rate without the differential. Understandably, Panamanians considered this move a violation of the 1955 pact, in spirit at least.

The situation deteriorated rapidly in the late 1950s, nor did Governor William E. Potter of the Canal Zone help matters with his hostile attitude. On November 3, 1959, some Panamanians walked into the Canal Zone with their flag and tried to unfurl it. A few hotheads antagonized the guards, and Governor Potter ordered his troops to fix bayonets. Thirty Panamanians were hospitalized. Potter added fuel to nationalist fires with his remarks after the fray, evoking the famous "Black Legend" stereotype of Spain and Latin America: "To an Anglo-Saxon, a contract is binding, but to a Spaniard a contract is only an extension of his personal ambitions. The Spaniard has an absolute lack of personal discipline. He thinks the law is a fine thing, but not applicable to him." [22] Panamanians, and all Latin Americans, bristled at these remarks. Despite her admiration for Ambassador Julian F. Harrington, who deplored Potter's actions, Panama now insisted upon these demands: (1) the implementation of the 1955 clause of equal pay for equal work; (2) the recognition of Panamanian sovereignty to the Canal Zone; and (3) the purchase, either from the United States or from Panama, of all products needed in the Canal Zone.

After the Potter incident the United States government was compelled to make one concession after another to wounded Panamanian sensitivities. President Eisenhower, at a press conference on December 2, 1959, recognized the need for some "visual evidence that Panama has titular sovereignty over that region." [23] In September 1960 Eisenhower ordered officials in the Canal Zone to arrange for a display of Panamanian sovereignty in accordance with the precedent set by Secretary of War Taft in 1906. President Kennedy continued his predecessor's policy. In June 1962, after a state visit to the United States by President Roberto F. Chiari, a joint commission was assigned to discuss the bones of contention between the two nations. A year later Panama and the United States agreed that their flags would be flown together in selected places within the Canal Zone. On

[22] New Haven *Evening Register*, November 11, 1959.
[23] *Arizona Daily Star* (Tucson), January 28, 1960.

December 30, 1963, the Governor of the Canal Zone, Robert J. Fleming, Jr., indicated the sites where the two flags would be displayed together and where the American flag would no longer be exhibited outdoors. Balboa High School was one of these locations. On January 7, 1964, students ignored Fleming's directive; two days later, Panamanian demonstrations led to bloodshed and the break in diplomatic relations between Panama and the United States. Fortunately, relations have been restored, but the wound is still wide open.

Latin Americans judged the Panama crisis of January 1964 not on its merits but in its historical perspective. The incident recalled moments in their own past history when the United States had acted toward them peremptorily and without regard for their feelings and aspirations. And it also brought to mind those occasions when citizens of the United States had treated them as racial and cultural inferiors.

To appreciate and understand the trends, developments, attitudes, and prospects of contemporary Central America, let us now turn to the various phases of her historical experience.

TWO

A Disunited Republic:

The Nineteenth Century

Central America has made a sovereign state of
each village.[1]

Domingo Faustino Sarmiento

At one time, following the pattern of the colonial administrative unit called the Captaincy General of Guatemala, Central
America formed a single political entity. From 1823 to 1839 the experiment in republicanism and union tried vainly to sink its roots
into the ground, until a swelling wave of states' rights sentiment
finally overpowered it. When Central American liberals struggled to
re-establish a republic by insisting on "a more perfect union," as had
happened in North America after the turbulent Articles of Confederation period, their efforts again floundered in the quagmire of Central American politics and the rivalry of Great Britain and the United
States for control of the interoceanic passageway through Nicaragua.
Thus the five present nations of Central America made good their
separate bids for independence and followed their swaggering *caudillos* into the modern world. The centrifugal tendencies of Central
American society had triumphed over the forces of modernization.
The traditional social order, however, was slightly altered in the
process.

[1] Alberto Herrarte, *La unión de Centro América: Tragedia y esperanza* (Guatemala, 1955), p. 137, quoting Sarmiento's "Centro América ha hecho un estado
soberano de cada aldea" (*Argirópolis*).

49

What is the explanation for Central America's failure to progress along republican lines during the key decades of nation building? Was it simply the consequence of Spain's despotic and obscurantist rule, as so many observers have claimed? Suffocated by a highly centralized regime and kept in ignorance of modern intellectual currents, so the argument runs, the ex-colonials stumbled and fell at every turn. Let us examine the validity of this explanation for the breakdown of order in Central America during the first part of the nineteenth century.

The Colonial Mentality

For all practical purposes, the conquest of Central America was over by 1545, leaving the *conquistador* free to implant the institutions of Western Europe, as forged on the Iberian Peninsula, in the New World. Always a minority in those new lands, the white man imposed his control over the natives, using every means known to him. With Draconian methods, only slightly tempered by the influence of followers of the Cross, the Spaniard subjugated the hostile and less civilized tribes of what is now Costa Rica, Nicaragua, Honduras, and El Salvador. He thoroughly assimilated or "ladinoized" them, a process that was undoubtedly aided by the white man's promiscuous relations with the Indian woman, producing the *mestizos*, or *ladinos*, of the colonial period. Discriminated against because of his illegitimate origin and mixed ancestry, the *mestizo's* position in society was not an enviable one, and it is not surprising that he frequently turned to vice and crime and thus further stigmatized his caste. The old established families made a fetish of preserving their racial purity, as befitted the military nature and rigid class structure of Western European society in the New World, a system in which mobility was the exception rather than the rule.

In Guatemala, by way of contrast, the Spaniard took into account and capitalized upon the Indians' passive resistance. He was unable to assimilate the descendants of the Mayas to any substantial degree. Their greater numbers precluded this, and, as today, they stubbornly preserved their own culture and languages. Colonial authority was eventually established over the Indians of Guatemala thanks to the efforts of the Spanish Church. In converting the Indians the missionaries realistically permitted them to practice a modified form of Christianity that absorbed many of the Old Mayan rituals. This fusion of religions can be seen today in such Guatemalan towns as Santo Tomás Chichicastenango.[2] Gradually, in return for the Indians' acceptance of Spanish rule, they were allowed to live in separate villages under the guidance of their elders, a parish priest, and a royal official called a *corregidor*.

The system had many advantages to recommend it. It could facilitate the religious training of the Indians, protect them from the abuse of the whites and *mestizos*, thus winning their nominal allegiance, and provide the necessary work force for colonial agriculture. The *corregidor*, for example, supervised the forced labor levies (*mandamientos*), of Indian workers so that the white masters would not abuse them. When numerous violations occurred, the government prohibited the forced labor of Indians. But the Crown's good intentions were not usually heeded. Local landowners had no trouble exploiting the Indians, oftentimes with the open collaboration of royal officials who might benefit personally from the operation. The *hacendado* was the undisputed master in his bailiwick. Priests and *corregidores*—the latter were not all corrupt—might persuade the *patrón* to be more benevolent and in some cases were able to bring him to justice, but by and large the *hacendado* ruled according to his own conscience, if he had one.

We can see, then, that Spain's control over her subjects in Central America was not so effective as is generally believed. This was true for several reasons. To begin with, the rough topography and inadequate internal communications as well as the enormous distance from Spain to Central America, militated against the establishment of a highly centralized system of government, a feat which would be difficult enough under modern conditions. Moreover, Spanish theory of government broke down in practice because the mother country depended upon her colonials to defend and hold the far-flung empire from the attacks of envious foreign nations; she simply did not have the resources nor the manpower to garrison the New World at her own expense. And so concessions had to be made to home rule,

[2] See Donald E. Thompson, *Maya Paganism and Christianity: A History of the Fusion of Two Religions* (New Orleans, 1954), pp. 5-35.

with the result that decentralization of power became characteristic —a development which perhaps helps to explain why the Spanish empire lasted as long as it did.[3]

It was at the municipal level (*cabildo* or *ayuntamiento*) that Spanish colonials had the greatest scope to express their will and gained considerable experience in self-government by resorting to various and ingenious techniques to circumvent the implementation of unpopular decrees and by usurping prerogatives of government which were clearly not theirs in theory. Except for a brief period at the very beginning, *cabildos* were not democratic institutions; on the contrary, they were controlled by, and for the benefit of, the local aristocracy. It was only the colonial elite—the *patrones* or *hacendados* we mentioned earlier—who learned the art of self-government, or perhaps we should say, of advancing and protecting their interests within the Spanish imperial system. In fact, it can be argued that *criollos* (Europeans born in the New World) enjoyed *too much* self-government during the colonial centuries—a more realistic explanation for the centrifugal tendencies of the early national period, as we shall see.

A concomitant of the decentralized imperial system was the *hacienda* (plantation), the key to the economic and social structure of colonial life. Partly feudal and partly capitalistic, the plantation was a self-sustaining unit in periods of economic decline and an instrument of commercial agriculture in better times, producing exports for the international market. Even during the colonial centuries the pattern of monoculture, with all of its weaknesses, characterized the economic system of Central America: the dependence upon food imports while the *hacienda* devoted its entire effort to producing cacao, indigo, cattle, and other export crops; the erratic fluctuations of world prices and competition from other sources of supply; the domestic debtor-creditor relationship; the reliance upon outside capital; and the chronic need for cheap transportation facilities.

Except for brief periods of activity, Central America's economic productivity was not considered too important in the total Spanish imperial scheme. Her population was relatively small; by 1800 there were from one half to one million people living in the area where the

---

[3] For a convincing exposition of this thesis see François Chevalier, *Land and Society in Colonial Mexico: The Great Hacienda* (Berkeley, 1963).

Maya civilization had once flourished—western Guatemala, north-western Honduras, and El Salvador. There was another population cluster in the Nicaraguan lowlands. Costa Rica was out of the way and of practically no significance to the Captaincy General of Guatemala. Her population was very small, and only a few whites cared to spend their lives there, eking out a bare existence and working with their own hands in the absence of Indian labor. In neighboring Nicaragua, upon which Costa Rica was dependent for administrative and fiscal purposes, the production of cacao had once been an important source of wealth for Nicaraguan landowners, but competition from areas bordering on the Caribbean, closer to the European market, eventually destroyed that lucrative trade. Honduras had suffered a similar fate with its mineral wealth, especially silver, because of transportation costs and the discovery of better deposits elsewhere in Spanish America. Both Nicaragua and Honduras, therefore, concentrated on the pastoral industry, selling their meat and by-products in El Salvador and western Guatemala.

During the eighteenth century the production of indigo, a blue dyestuff, became Central America's principal export and the basis for an extensive intraregional commerce that was to have important political repercussions. Although indigo had been grown since the end of the Conquest, the world's textile revolution increased the demand for it in the eighteenth century. Here was a product that commanded a high price and was light enough to minimize the transportation costs to the Caribbean coast from the centers of production located in El Salvador, western Guatemala, and, to a lesser extent, Nicaragua. Since most of Central America's people lived in El Salvador and Guatemala, the natural and most efficient trade route for the indigo traffic was via Guatemala City to the Atlantic port of Santo Tomás, near modern Puerto Barrios, founded in 1605. Political considerations also favored this route. As the capital of the Captaincy General, Guatemala City was the logical site to hold the annual indigo fairs, permitting royal officials to supervise the exchange of products and collect the tax revenues on this trade.[4]

[4] On this topic see the excellent articles by Troy S. Floyd, "The Guatemalan Merchants, the Government, and the *Provincianos*, 1750-1800," *Hispanic American Historical Review*, Vol. XLI, No. 1 (February 1961), 90-110; and Robert

Based upon indigo, the colonial common market worked satisfactorily during the first half of the eighteenth century. Salvadoreans and Guatemalans concentrated on growing indigo and depended upon Nicaraguans and Hondurans to supply them with the meat and foodstuffs to feed their workers. In this regional complex the large entrepreneurs came to dominate the traffic in their respective commodities. The wealthy indigo planter, for example, bought indigo from smaller growers and then, by mulepack, took the product to the fair in Guatemala City, where he exchanged it for specie, manufactured goods, and sundry items. Upon returning home he disposed of his wares in the local market. Large cattlemen followed the same procedure. Guatemala City merchants, who had contacts in Cádiz in southern Spain, purchased the indigo and meat from the *provincianos*, supplied them with the necessary manufactured goods, and provided them with capital. As long as times were prosperous, the regional arrangement seemed to satisfy everyone concerned. Undoubtedly this economic interdependence contributed to a general awareness of regional identity.

But during the 1770s and 1780s the *provincianos* became dissatisfied with the arrangement for one reason or another, feeling that they were being victimized by greedy "middlemen" and "monopolists" in Guatemala City. Whether they were justified or not is beside the point; the fact is that they resented their creditors in Guatemala City, and in the various petitions which they presented to the captain general in Guatemala City and to authorities in Spain they clamored for reforms. This is an excellent illustration of colonials exercising self-government of an economic nature.

The Spanish government, under the Bourbon dynasty, was not indifferent to the grievances of the *provincianos*, especially from 1779 to 1783 while Spain was again at war with England. Captain General Matías de Gálvez took steps to meet the colonials' demands during those years, and the Bourbon ministers in Spain followed suit with a series of reforms whose major objective was to undermine the Cádiz-Guatemala City monopolists. These new measures included plans for additional routes across Central America to the At-

S. Smith, "Indigo Productions and Trade in Colonial Guatemala," *Hispanic American Historical Review*, Vol. XXXIX, No. 2 (May 1959), 181-211.

lantic coast, the formation of a regional junta of indigo growers authorized to set prices for indigo in cooperation with the proper governmental officials, provision for credit facilities so that the *provincianos* would not have to depend upon Guatemalan merchants, and annual fairs to be held in El Salvador.

Despite the good intentions of the Spanish government, the above-mentioned reforms did not succeed in eliminating the real advantages of the Cádiz-Guatemala City route nor the determination of vested interests in the capital to maintain their position. Gálvez' successor, as it turned out, found it advantageous to himself to thwart the royal will, and agents favorable to Guatemala City supervised the new fairs in El Salvador. The net effect of the reforms, therefore, was to exacerbate the resentment of the *provincianos* toward the authority at Guatemala City, be it political or economic. This attitude of hostility, a psychological fact of no mean importance for the future, helps to explain the series of revolts and uprisings in Central America from 1808 forward, representing a defiance of Guatemala City's supremacy.

According to recent studies the *criollos'* education was comparable to that offered in European universities.[5] At the Universidad de San Carlos, founded at Antigua in 1676 and later moved to Guatemala City after the earthquake of 1773, colonial students were exposed to the intellectual tradition of scholasticism. And during the Enlightenment, thanks to such monarchs as Charles III of Spain (1759-88), rationalism gradually superseded the older approach to knowledge. Distinguished faculty members—many of them *criollos*, incidentally —brought about this transformation. José Felipe Flores, a native of Chiapas, specialized in surgery and was known the world over for his innovations. A Franciscan friar born in Costa Rica, José Antonio Liendo y Goicoechea, infused his students at San Carlos with a deep respect for the experimental approach to science and encouraged them to develop a social conscience. This great savant explored the economic and social problems of Central America with realism and humanity in his famous "Memorial on Mendicity."

[5] See the works of John Tate Lanning: *The University in the Kingdom of Guatemala* (Ithaca, 1955) and *The Eighteenth-Century Enlightenment in the University of San Carlos de Guatemala* (Ithaca, 1956).

There were many other notable participants in the intellectual renaissance in the Captaincy General of Guatemala during the 1790s and early decades of the nineteenth century. There existed in Central America during that period an enlightened public opinion aided and exemplified by such journals as the *Gazeta de Guatemala* and such organizations as the Economic Society of Friends of the Country. The future leaders of the Republic were indeed adequately trained, and their approach to new ideas and reforms was eclectic and pragmatic. They were by no means doctrinaire or dependent upon poorly digested fragments from the smuggled writings of French thinkers of the Enlightenment—the standard view of older works on the Spanish empire. If these leaders failed to establish effective republican institutions, it was not due to any lack of training or knowledge on their part. The causes of instability in Central America go much deeper than that.

"Dios, Unión, Libertad" (1808-1824)

"God, Union, Liberty," the motto of the Central American Republic, reflects succinctly and realistically the aspirations of the founding fathers at the time of independence from Spain. The constitution of November 22, 1824, with its commitment to the Catholic religion, could not have been otherwise in view of the role played by clerics in the independence movement. Since 1808, when the Guatemala City *cabildo* petitioned the Spanish government to fill the vacant archbishop's seat with a *criollo* (a request which was not granted), religious men, born in the New World, had been actively engaged in the movement for greater colonial autonomy. Leaders of the independence movement realized the importance of a modern and enlightened Church to bind together the citizens of the new nation. That there was strength in unity was a truism which the founding fathers accepted; without union the experiment in republicanism would lack the resources and population to form a modern nation capable of commanding respect in the world. And liberty would give the individual his chance to regenerate and create a better life for himself, his family, and his country. These were cherished ideals worth fighting for, but in achieving them Central Americans faced problems of formidable proportions, many of which derived from the colonial experience described above. The beginnings of disintegration were already evident in 1808, when European events initiated the movement for independence.

The abduction of Spain's royal family and Napoleon's insistence that his brother Joseph occupy the Spanish throne touched off the demonstrations of May 2, 1808, in Madrid, beginning the "War of Independence" from the French yoke. Of the regional bodies formed throughout the Peninsula to rule in the absence of Ferdinand VII, the *Junta Central* eventually prevailed. In January 1810 it gave way to the Regency of five men that called the constituent assembly of Cádiz in September, empowered to draw up a basic charter for the Spanish nation. This *Cortes* of Cádiz, operating from the nearby Isle of León, ran the government until the end of the Napoleonic Wars. Its greatest achievement was the enactment of the famous constitution of 1812, an eminently liberal charter. But Ferdinand VII, who was restored to his throne in 1814, rejected the constitution and asserted his autocratic will upon the nation and its empire. In January 1820 Colonel Rafael Riego rebelled against his monarch and forced him to restore the 1812 document. Three years later a French expeditionary force invaded Spain, and Ferdinand again became autocrat over his domains. All these events had important repercussions overseas, providing the impetus and context for the independence of most of Hispanic America.

In Central America the news of Ferdinand's abduction had the effect of straining imperial ties by fanning the latent hostility between *criollos* and the Iberian-born. To colonials the time seemed opportune to reaffirm their control of local governments and to defy the Spanish hierarchy in their midst. Since Creoles had been trusted with only minor posts in the governmental and religious hierarchies, the agitation took on an "American" versus "European" complexion. The attitude and actions of leading Spanish officials irritated many colonials. Fearful of French subversion—at least that was the alleged reason—the Captain General of Guatemala, Antonio González Mollinedo y Saravia, abolished freedom of the press and speech and jailed those persons whom he suspected of having treasonous ideas. For this purpose he established a special loyalty board (*Tribunal de Fidelidad*) on May 27, 1810, encharged with the investigation of subversive cases. All three judges were peninsulars. Creoles in general, and the *cabildo* of Guatemala City in particular, understandably complained of the implication that they were not loyal to the Crown and demanded equal representation for themselves on the special tribunal. In 1811 José de Bustamante assumed the post of captain general and for a brief period pursued a tact of compromise, thus at least temporarily relieving the situation.

Aware of this tension overseas, and fearful that *criollos* might elect to seek independence, the *Junta Central* issued an order in 1809 for the election of a delegate to represent Central America at its deliberations. Following a complicated procedure whereby the 15 major town governments in the Captaincy General suggested candidates for the position, a special board in Guatemala City made the final selection: Manuel Pavón, a prominent Creole merchant of the capital. Pavón never served on the *Junta Central* because it was soon replaced by the Regency. But the important thing is that a select number of *ayuntamientos* had participated in the regional elections, thus awakening their desire for home rule within the empire.

Early in 1810 the Regency sent out a new order calling for the election of a delegate from each of the six municipalities in the Captaincy General that were ranked as "heads of provinces" and allowing each province to instruct its representative on the type of government it wanted the *Cortes* of Cádiz to create. The following cities, most of which became the initial capitals of the future Central American countries, were authorized to hold elections: San Salvador (El Salvador), Comayagua (Honduras), León (Nicaragua), Cartago (Costa Rica), Guatemala City (Guatemala), and Ciudad Real (Chiapas). All six delegates from the Captaincy General of Guatemala signed the constitution of 1812, though they did not arrive in Spain until the final discussions on that famous document. Nevertheless, in accordance with their instructions, the representatives of Central America were in full accord with the principles adopted at Cádiz. They favored proportional representation, home rule for the provinces, the abolition of special privileges and monopolies, an enlightened economic policy, a sound and equitable tax system, and the review and modernization of Spanish laws. The *criollos*, at this time, were liberal, at least in their intellectual orientation. As it later turned out, many colonials of a conservative bent were merely interested in home rule and had no intentions of adopting modern, liberal institutions.

The constitution of 1812 embodied an amazing experiment of imperial reorganization which might have prevented independence if other factors had not impinged. Following the principle of proportional representation, the former Kingdom (*Reino*) of Guatemala was authorized to elect twelve deputies to the Spanish parliament. Moreover, the Cádiz charter outlawed the old oligarchical practices of buying offices and prescribed a complex but workable system of popular and indirect elections for positions in municipal governments and for the two regional bodies (*diputaciones provinciales*): one centered at León which included the modern countries of Nicaragua and Costa Rica and the other at Guatemala City, encompassing what is today the Mexican state of Chiapas and the nations of El Salvador, Honduras, and Guatemala. The *jefe politico* (political chief) of Nicaragua was an appointee of the Spanish government, subject to the authority of the *jefe politico superior* in Guatemala City. Rather than regional political units in the modern sense, the *disputaciones provinciales* were similar to development corporations of the present day. In short, the Spain of 1812 was willing to give her subjects overseas a more democratic and representative form of government. Although these reforms failed, it is indeed significant that subsequent national governments of Central America adopted the terminology and even the system outlined in the constitution of 1812.

Captain General José Bustamante was largely responsible for the failure of this experiment. During 1811, the first year of his tenure, he pursued a statesmanlike policy toward colonial uprisings despite his lack of sympathy with the liberal climate of opinion in Spain. The insurrection of San Salvador in November 1811 is a case in point. The motivation for that uprising was both personal and sectional. In the instructions to their delegate at Cádiz the leaders of San Salvador had urged the establishment of a bishopric in their province, reflecting a desire for religious autonomy and freedom from the archbishop of Guatemala City and for equality with the cities of Ciudad Real, León, and Comayagua, which had bishoprics. Father José Matías Delgado, whose relatives were powerful in the *cabildo* of San Salvador, aspired to that position. His family, including his nephew Manuel José Arce, who became the first president of the Central American Republic, headed the revolt of November 1811. It was a dismal failure. The reasons for this are significant, for they illustrate the exaggerated form of self-government that prevailed during colonial times. From envy of San Salvador and to appease the ambition of their own ruling families, the municipalities of Santa Ana, San Miguel, and San Vicente refused to support the uprising at the capital. Moreover, Bustamante and his advisors in Guatemala City wisely encouraged this refusal by promising to upgrade the status of their governments in the hierarchy of town and city rankings and by granting choice appointments to the Molinas of San Vicente, the Barroetas of San Miguel, and the Cárcamos of Santa Ana. In addition, Bustamante sent two prominent Creoles from Guatemala City to serve as peace emissaries; one of them replaced the Spanish-born intendant, who presumably had abused his authority at San Salvador. A contemporary revolt in León, Nicaragua, was also handled judiciously by the Captain General, but this cannot be said for the uprising in Granada of late 1811 and early 1812. In this case he adopted harsh measures, determined to make an example of the Granadians.

Actually, the change in Bustamante's tactics resulted from the growing conviction that the dangerous example set by Father Miguel Hidalgo and Father José María Morelos in Mexico had to be discouraged in the Captaincy General of Guatemala. Many *criollos*, incidentally, shared his apprehensions. The possibility of a "War of the Castes" was a factor which brought fear to the minds of squabbling whites and compelled them on many occasions to settle their differences. An uprising of the Indians or *mestizos* was no laughing matter; the massacre which attended Father Hidalgo's movement in 1810 never left their minds. Thus, many leading Creoles like José Cecilio del Valle from Honduras sanctioned *el terror bustamantino*, which lasted until 1818.[6] Moreover, Captain General Bustamante chafed under the new provincial system of the 1812 constitution

[6] See Louis E. Bumgartner, *José del Valle of Central America* (Durham, 1963), and Franklin D. Parker, *José Cecilio del Valle and the Establishment of the Central American Confederation* (Tegucigalpa, 1954).

and refused to accept any advice from the *diputación provincial* or the popularly elected *cabildo* of Guatemala City. His arbitrary ways produced more uprisings: the so-called Belén Conspiracy of 1813 in Guatemala City and a second revolt in San Salvador in early 1814. When Ferdinand VII repealed the provincial experiment in government, the movement for independence from Spain gained headway.

The Riego revolt and the subsequent restoration of the 1812 constitution convinced all Central Americans that the time for independent action was at hand. Although Creole liberals sympathized with the constitution of 1812, they knew that its reforms could always be vitiated by men like Bustamante, and they preferred the establishment of a separate republic. Creole conservatives, on the other hand, wanted to keep political power in their own hands—an objective which did not envision liberal reforms of any type, regardless of origin. And Creole moderates, who did not share the liberals' faith in republican institutions, felt that the time was ripe to join the Plan of Iguala in Mexico, which proposed to establish a Mexican empire headed by a member of the Bourbon dynasty in Spain.

For varying reasons the Mexican project appealed to most Central Americans, leaving the liberals without much support for an experiment in republicanism. By joining the Mexican empire the *provincianos* of Central America hoped to shake off the onerous control of Guatemala City on the assumption that this would permit them more self-rule. Mexico City, after all, was farther away. On August 28, 1821, the province of Chiapas initiated the *provincianos'* movement to join the Plan of Iguala—an action which was never reversed, thus explaining why Chiapas is now a Mexican state rather than an independent Central American country.

To counter Chiapas secession and to prevent any further defections in the former Captaincy General, both liberal and conservative interests in Guatemala City favored the Declaration of Independence on September 15, 1821. The big question now was whether to set up a republic, as the liberals wanted, or to join the Mexican empire, which had fallen into the ambitious hands of Agustín de Iturbide, now the self-styled Emperor Agustín I. The *provincianos* preferred the imperial connection; so did the conservative and moderate Creoles in Guatemala City. Yet the unanimity of opinion—except for the liberals

—was deceiving. Whereas the *provincianos* wanted to join Mexico in order to liberate themselves from the grasp of Guatemala City, interests in Guatemala hoped to maintain the hegemony of their city within the Mexican empire.

The tradition of decentralization and exaggerated local control of colonial days burst upon the Central American stage with the fury of a tornado, making stability of government almost an impossibility. Comayagua declared for the Plan of Iguala on September 28, 1821; so did León and Cartago, and also Quezaltenango, representing the highlands of present Guatemala that wanted no part of a government centered in Guatemala City. San Salvador, on the other hand, declared her independence from all domination on September 29, 1821. And it was not just the provinces rebelling against Guatemala City. Within the provinces themselves disintegration was rampant. Granada opposed León; Tegucigalpa opposed Comayagua; San José opposed Cartago. President Sarmiento of Argentina was not far from the truth when he said that every Central American village had declared its sovereignty. The colonial heritage had indeed left its telltale marks upon the area.

Central America's annexation to Mexico was of short duration. As Iturbide's empire began to crumble and Mexican troops made themselves unpopular by repressing the Salvadoreans, who sought to annex themselves to the United States, the liberals of Central America seized the initiative and set under way the establishment of a republic. On June 29, 1823, a national constituent assembly in Guatemala City declared its "absolute independence" from all domination, and during the next 16 months this body, sharing power with a provisional executive of three men, drafted a charter for the new nation and passed a series of enlightened decree-laws and projects that demonstrated conclusively the capacity of these ex-colonials to govern themselves. Although initially the liberals took charge of the provisional government, the assembly's complexion changed as the conservatives of the capital city and of the provinces, recognizing the inevitable, decided to join the government. The constitution of November 22, 1824, was not therefore the exclusive handiwork of liberals, as so many commentators have implied. Rather, it was a compromise document that attempted to reconcile different political aspirations.

The founding fathers of Central America had to contend with a serious dilemma. The *provinciano* preferred a loosely organized confederation, one which would allow him to control his own area and at the same time prevent the former capital of Guatemala City from dominating him. Yet how could a weak government of this type hope to implement reforms that would modernize Central America in accord with the ideas of the Enlightenment? Alone, the states lacked the population and resources to protect themselves and pay for the reforms and projects needed to raise their level of education and standard of living. With hindsight we can easily say that Central Americans should have chosen a unitary or centralized form of government to get their republican experiment going. Yet how would a plan of this sort have fared in the light of prevailing conditions and the historical conditioning of Central Americans? Such a constitution would never have gotten off the drawing board; a compromise was the only hope.

In drawing up the basic charter Central Americans, as might be expected, were strongly influenced by the Cádiz constitution of 1812, though they also had at hand the United States document of 1789, the Colombian federal and unitary plans of government, the Portuguese constitution, and the French governmental codes. The result was a blend that appeared suitable to the Central American environment. In imitation of the Cádiz document, the main organ of sovereignty was the Chamber of Deputies, elected by the "people" according to the principle of proportional representation. The Senate, consisting of two representatives from each state, resembled the colonial *audiencia* in that it partook of both executive and advisory functions, having a limited veto power over the acts of the Chamber and serving in its place during a recess, somewhat like an advisory council to the president. The executive and judicial branches of government had limited powers and were subject to control by the legislature. Ideas of constitutional monarchy were reflected in these and other features of the 1824 charter in recollection of how Bustamante had thwarted the constitution of 1812. Many prominent liberals, especially José Francisco Barrundia, felt that a powerless executive would weaken the new government. But the general consensus, including conservatives from the provinces, was that a safeguard was necessary. Although universal suffrage was the accepted principle, all officials of the national government were to be elected by a complicated electoral college system, apparently with the view of preventing demagogues from riding into power on the votes of the masses.

The constitution called for a similar framework of government at the state level: a *jefe político* elected by the people, an advisory council resembling the *diputación provincial*, and a one-house legislature—all selected by popular vote. Article 10 declared that the states were "free and independent" insofar as their interior administration was concerned, a troublesome clause which subsequently led to friction between the states and the national government.

Controversy has raged over whether the constitution of 1824 established a "confederation" or league of states on the one hand, or a "federation" or unitary republic on the other. Actually, the constitution had provisions which justify either thesis, underscoring the compromise of the two positions during the debates of the constituent assembly. Whereas Article 10 supported the states' rights thesis, Article 69 made the national congress responsible for enacting unified substantive law—that is, all states were required to enforce the criminal, civil, and commercial codes drawn up by the national legislature. From the nationalist point of view, Article 10 merely gave the states authority in what is called administrative law. Other prerogatives of the constitution, permitting the central government to act directly upon all citizens, make it clear that the founding fathers, in theory at least, intended a federation. In this respect, therefore, the constitution of 1824 was more nationalistic than the United States constitution of 1789.

But the fact was something else again. Since the federal congress never finished the various codes called for in Article 69, and because of the unsettled state of affairs during the life of the Republic, the states framed their own laws and developed a tradition of independence which was unconstitutional in theory, thus setting the scene for a states' rights controversy that brought about the dissolution of the Republic.

How was it possible to make the constitution so nationalistic in view of the undisguised suspicions that the *provincianos* entertained about Guatemala City? Before answering this question, let us consider the following points. The constitution makers had no exact notion of the vital statistics of Central America, and one of the first things they did was to appoint a commission to determine and to survey the population and resources of the area. In the meantime the constituent assembly worked out a compromise formula on population in order to arrange the composition of the first national congress, which opened its sessions in February 1825. Estimating the population of the country at 1,270,000, and following the ratio of one deputy for every 30,000 inhabitants, the make-up of that congress was as follows: Guatemala had 18 deputies; El Salvador, 9; Honduras, 6; Nicaragua, 6; and Costa Rica, 2. Clearly, the principle of proportional representation worked in Guatemala's favor. In addition, Guatemalan representatives shrewdly introduced a proposal, which was passed, permitting the election of delegates-at-large. They argued that limiting the election of delegates to those born in a given district might not bring forth the best qualified candidates; moreover, the burdensome expense of traveling to the national capital from the outlying states was another factor favoring this practice.

Were the *provincianos* that naïve? No, they were not. After all, they outnumbered Guatemala in the Senate, and they could still offset her advantage in the legislature, provided they could cooperate among themselves. They had no intention of allowing Guatemala City to be the national capital. The constitution implied that the capital would be elsewhere, the delegates-at-large technique could work in their favor also. Finally, in the absence of correct statistics they had reason to believe that they could minimize Guatemala City's influence by creating a new state from the highlands area around Quezaltenango, which, it will be recalled, shared the *provincianos'* distaste for Guatemala City. And if Chiapas returned to the fold, as many expected she would, then Guatemala City would be cut down to size, on a par with every other state of the union. That is why *provincianos* sanctioned the nationalistic features of the 1824 constitution. The national charter, in fact, was popular in most sectors of Central America for its enlightened concepts and vision of the future.

The Experiment in Unionism (1824-1839)

Optimism and euphoria prevailed at the first national congress in February 1825. The economic depression that preceded independence had abated because cochineal, another dyestuff, replaced indigo as the leading export and brought higher prices. By welcoming foreign immigrants with their know-how and capital, it was hoped that Central America might be able to establish a sound economic base. And there were indications that such optimism was well founded: George Thompson, an English agent, was surveying the area's resources for his country's information, and banking houses were competing keenly for the opportunity to loan the Republic money. Much of the economic upswing and stability from 1823 to 1826 was due to the enlightened projects initiated by the provisional triumvirate that included the Honduran savant, José Cecilio del Valle, who was well known for his knowledge of political economy.[7] If the trend had continued a few more years, Central America's history might have been otherwise.

But the political honeymoon did not last long. Civil war broke out in 1826 and tore the country apart for three important years. Unwilling to submit to congressional restrictions, President Manuel José Arce, a Salvadorean liberal of the preindependence period, turned against his fellow liberals and aligned himself with the conservatives of Guatemala City, who were willing to suffer his personal ambitions in return for gaining control of their state government. To the ex-*provincianos* this could mean only one thing: that the interests of Guatemala City, the so-called *serviles*, aimed to dominate the political and economic life of the new nation as they had done in colonial days. Behind the banner of constitutionalism—to preserve the constitution of 1824 from its first President and from their own sectional rivals—the ex-provincials fought for their cause on the battlefield.

During the course of this bitter struggle the ideological issues came to the fore. Showing their contempt for liberal institutions, the *serviles* of Guatemala City, led by the Marquis de Aycinena, restored many anachronistic colonial practices. Supporting Aycinena were

[7] Parker, *op. cit.*, pp. 59-62; Bumgartner, *op. cit.*, pp. 232-35.

many prominent churchmen of the colonial hierarchy, Spaniards by birth. Thus, the Church-state issue, which had not caused any trouble at the time of independence for reasons which we have mentioned, now came to the surface and inflamed the minds of many liberals. The ideological impact of the civil war from 1826 to 1829 was not soon to be forgotten; it permeated Central American history throughout the nineteenth century.

Thanks to the military genius of Francisco Morazán, a Honduran, the war ended in April 1829. When the congress reconvened on June 22, 1829, the victorious liberals, of course, dominated the national government and all of the state regimes. Despite the efforts of responsible liberal leaders, who recognized that vindictive measures toward the vanquished might further distract the nation and prolong its recovery, congressmen decided to exile prominent *serviles*, including the Aycinenas and Archbishop Ramón Casaus y Torres, and to expropriate the properties of the Church. These punitive acts fanned the resistance of the opposition and prompted two attempts at invasion from Mexican and Caribbean bases. Not until 1831, after five years of constant warfare and hostility, was the nation able to rest.

The Central American Republic never recovered from the consequences of those five years. With the economy ruined and the federal debt approaching five million *pesos*, the Republic could not even meet its normal administrative expenses, let alone pay off its obligations to foreign bondholders. In December 1825 the House of Barclay had agreed to float a loan of eight million *pesos* in the English market, but a few years later, the house went bankrupt, and Central American bonds dropped in value—those that had been sold. And what little money had come into the coffers of the Republic was soon squandered by the Arce government. All that was left was the obligation to the Bondholders Association and to the Reid-Irving Company, which had assumed responsibility for paying the expenses of the diplomatic mission to England and the early dividends and interest to bondholders. The liberals duly acknowledged these obligations upon returning to power.[8]

[8] For an excellent analysis see Robert S. Smith, "Financing the Central American Federation, 1821-1838," *Hispanic American Historical Review*, Vol. XLIII, No. 4 (November 1963), 483-510.

After five years of constant fighting, during which the state gov
ernments acquired habits of fiscal independence and managed their
own affairs, the Republic understandably found it difficult to get any
more money from its defenders; they were financially prostrate too. In
fact, during the long struggle they had taken over federal tariff
revenues and especially the tobacco tax, and they were not willing to
give them up. On the contrary, the Republic was called upon to
surrender the tobacco monopoly in 1833, though it was returned
three years later. To argue that a centralized financial system might
have saved the day in Central America is to ignore the realities of
the 1830s.

To President Francisco Morazán, who began his first term in 1830,
it was patently clear that his constituents wanted constitutional reforms and that the compromise of 1824 had presumed a national consciousness that did not exist. At any rate, the states were in no mood
to countenance the unitary features of the constitution any longer.
The national government, hoping to preserve the union, therefore
encouraged and welcomed treatises that suggested amendments to
the constitution. The position taken by unionists like Morazán and
his close advisor José Francisco Barrundia was that the presidency
should be strengthened, the judiciary given tenure of office to maintain its independence as a third branch of the government, the
suffrage limited, and a balance struck between the powers of the
states and the federal government. The establishment of a federal
district was also a desired reform. In other words, they advocated
the example of the United States, whose constitution blended
harmoniously the states' rights and nationalistic principles, and it is
significant that the *Federalist Papers* circulated, in translation, during
the debates on constitutional reform. This unionist viewpoint inspired the 1835 amendments, which were agreed to by the federal
congress but which failed to get the required two-thirds vote of each
of the five states, though a majority favored the amendments.

The exaggerated localism of the colonial period also plagued the
existence of the Republic, for intrastate rivalries continued to intrude
themselves upon the national scene. At times these were merely
struggles between gangs of politicians fighting for the spoils of office.
More often they reflected the ideological clash of liberal versus con-

servative or unionists against states' righters, and on yet other occasions they were traditional feuds between rival municipalities for control of the state government. Whenever federal forces intervened to restore order, they gained the hatred of interested elements in that state; this in turn heightened the demand for states' rights, the federal government, in the meantime, being saddled with the expense of intervention. The levying of forced loans, which was the only way the Republic could raise money, antagonized the monied interests throughout Central America and discouraged economic activity, especially since there was not much likelihood of repayment. Thus, defiance of the Republic was commonplace; the government simply did not have the resources to command respect or to fulfill its obligations to the states.

Actually, the Republic could not have survived without the financial and physical assistance of the liberal government of Guatemala under Governor Mariano Gálvez (1831-38). It was during his incumbency that Guatemala became a model of educational, economic, and legal reforms. He sponsored the introduction of Edward Livingston's penal codes in Guatemala, a system that Livingston had drawn up for the state of Louisiana and that embodied progressive legal principles. Governor Gálvez also negotiated contracts with English entrepreneurs to exploit and colonize the northern frontier of his state, bordering on what is now British Honduras. His state was the only one to meet its financial obligations to the Republic, and his military aid helped to maintain a modicum of respect for the federal authorities, which, until 1834, resided in Guatemala City.

But the Livingston codes, which went into effect in Guatemala on January 1, 1837, produced a disastrous split in the liberal ranks and paved the way for the final secessionist movement in Central America. Largely responsible for translating the codes and adapting them to the conditions in his native state, José Francisco Barrundia looked forward to a judicial system that embodied trial by jury and made judges responsible to legislative authority. Moreover, if implemented, the codes would have decentralized political power within the state by giving the departments elected sheriffs rather than a *jefe político* appointed by the governor in Guatemala City.

At first, Governor Gálvez encouraged and welcomed the experiment, which worked satisfactorily among the West European elements in the vicinity of the state capital. The results were ludicrous, however, in the zones where Indians did not speak Spanish. And when Gálvez' partisans realized the political implications of the experiment, they demanded the suspension of the codes. Faced with a cholera epidemic of alarming proportions, Governor Gálvez met this request. But Barrundia attributed this move to base political considerations and launched a "War of Principles" against his erstwhile cohort.[9]

The dissension between Barrundia and Gálvez could not have come at a more inopportune time—the cholera epidemic that broke out in Belize in 1836 and soon invaded El Salvador and Guatemala. To prevent the spread of the disease Gálvez ordered *cordones* placed around the infected areas and enlisted the aid of all persons with medical knowledge to care for the sick and to help with preventive measures. The situation was grave, and the Indians were in a state of panic, desperately seeking every avenue of escape and unable to comprehend the quarantine measures of their government. Aggravating matters even more, certain overzealous clergymen, who could not forgive the liberals for weakening the power of the Church, convinced the terrified Indians that the Gálvez government was determined to eliminate them all by sending doctors to poison their drinking water. According to these malicious wags the *Galvecistas* had passed the recent tax law and had granted lands in the public domain to friends of the government in order to deprive the Indians of their means of livelihood; all these measures, they maintained, were part of a plan to turn over the country to heretics—the Englishmen who had recently arrived in Guatemala in connection with the colonization project.

Angry at these reports and frantic with fear, the Indians openly defied the government, leaving Governor Gálvez no alternative but to declare martial law and to assume extraordinary powers. Since the Indians associated the Livingston experiment with the new tax law —the same personnel set up the courts and conducted inventories of their possessions—Gálvez considered it expedient to suspend the codes. Maintaining that the cholera epidemic was no longer a threat,

---

[9] For a detailed evaluation see my study *The Livingston Codes in the Guatemalan Crisis of 1837-1838* (New Orleans, 1955).

Barrundia charged that Gálvez' dictatorial powers were unconstitutional, that the Governor merely wanted to assure the victory of his partisans in the fall elections.

From the cholera epidemic of 1837 and the split between Barrundia and Gálvez emerged a new factor in Guatemalan politics, the use of the masses as a political instrument of power. The Indian chieftain—some say he was a *mestizo*—Rafael Carrera destined to become the master *caudillo* of Central America, entered the pages of history at this time. This natural leader of men, the "King of the Indians," as his admirers called him, a master of guerrilla warfare who commanded the blind allegiance of both Indians and *mestizos*—Rafael Carrera rose to prominence because Guatemalan liberals were divided, because the *serviles* saw in him a device that would permit them to recover political control of their state, and because the "barbarian" threatened to unleash his "hordes" on the white population if he did not get his way. The ex-muleteer was given his first real opportunity by the liberals themselves. Determined to drive Gálvez out of office, Barrundia joined with Carrera in the military action of January 1838, a foolish alliance that the great Guatemalan ideologist would live to regret. And since General Morazán and other federal leaders could not defeat Carrera decisively, the chieftain was able to consolidate his power. His survival, moreover, was disastrous for the Republic, since it encouraged the states' righters throughout Central America to defy the central government with impunity. The Republic's days were numbered.

These were the conditions that gave rise to the last effort to save the union by reforming the constitution of 1824—the secession crisis of 1838 and early 1839. After the defeat of the 1835 amendments the federal congress empowered President Morazán to resume the tobacco monopoly and to recommend fiscal reforms. The result of this was the 1837 tariff and a new customs law which was to go into effect in January 1838. Congress, in other words, put unionism to the greatest test, that of the pocketbook. Without fiscal soundness the Republic was a chimera. Unionists voted for the measure; so did the states' righters, knowing full well that it would probably bring down the Republic. And it did. In April 1838 Nicaragua seceded from the union; she had no intention of giving up her port revenues to the Republic, and if a canal were to be constructed through her territory—various offers to do this had been presented—she wanted the revenues all for herself. If there was any consciousness of Central Americanism in Nicaragua at that time, it was nothing more than an oratorical device. Nicaraguans maintained that their secession was temporary; if the federal congress of 1838 reformed the constitution, they would return to the fold.

With the defeat of Governor Gálvez in January 1838 it appeared that the reform movement might succeed. One of the major complaints of the states was that Guatemala had too much power in the federal government and that the original idea of forming two states from that area had been frustrated by both conservative and liberal groups in Guatemala City. And this was true. Gálvez did not permit Los Altos to petition the federal government for statehood. Understandably, the Quezaltenango interests backed Barrundia in his controversy with Gálvez, not because they were sincerely interested in the enlightened principles of the Livingston experiment but because it permitted more autonomy to the highlands. When Gálvez fell, Los Altos immediately asked for statehood, and it was granted by the federal authorities. Central America now had six states, thus satisfying one of the major grievances of the smaller states.

Despite this favorable omen and the federal government's sincere measures to reform the constitution during the sessions of the 1838 congress, compromising almost to the danger point, the fact is that states' righters were bent upon independence and rejected the compromises.[10] *Caudillos*—Carrera in Guatemala, Braulio Carrillo in Costa Rica, Francisco Ferrera in Honduras—wanted unlimited power for themselves. Conservatives felt that the time was ripe to upset liberalism at both the national and state levels, and states' rights liberals were apparently interested only in the spoils of office. To be sure, they rationalized their defection and lack of nationalism by charging that the *Morazanistas* were power-mad—it takes one to recognize one, as the old saying goes—and that they were not willing to hold a convention to consider reforms. On the contrary, after

[10] Mario Rodríguez, A *Palmerstonian Diplomat in Central America: Frederick Chatfield, Esq.* (Tucson, 1964), pp. 151-61. I wish to thank the University of Arizona Press for allowing me to paraphrase sections of this study.

passing amendments similar to those of 1835 the federal congress also proposed a convention of state delegations empowered to recommend further reforms to the constitution. To prevent this convention from running away by drawing up a document that would establish a loose confederation, the unionists insisted on certain safeguards: the document would be presented to the next federal congress, scheduled to meet in February 1839; if the congress approved, the reforms would go into effect immediately; if not, the next step would be to call a national constituent assembly. But the states' righters wanted no part of this compromise offer, and Rafael Carrera's disturbing presence in Guatemala encouraged other states to secede. By the end of 1838 Costa Rica and Honduras had joined Nicaragua in the secessionist column, and it was an open secret that the latter two states were preparing an invasion of El Salvador. The so-called Allied States signed treaties, of an offensive nature, in January 1839.

Only two states remained faithful to the union in the early months of 1839: Los Altos, whose future depended upon the continuation of the federal government, and El Salvador, where federal authorities resided. To placate the secessionists, President Morazán resigned from office in early February, and the federal government issued one last call for a convention. The Allied States answered this plea for unity by invading El Salvador—a challenge that General Morazán met with energy and decision, routing the forces of Francisco Ferrera. But the states' rights position gained a new lease on life in April 1839 when Carrera occupied Guatemala City and his sponsors, the *serviles*, declared the independence of their state from the union.

The Central American Republic perished in February 1839 with Morazán's resignation from the presidency. Since the states had not held elections the previous fall, there was no legislature, just a few caretaker officials of the executive branch. Central America's experiment in unionism was over, a dismal failure. Yet its memory has endured to the present.

A Stranger in Their Midst

Perhaps it is a sense of guilt that compels many Central Americans to seek a scapegoat for the failure of union: that irascible *extrangero* Frederick Chatfield, Great Britain's "Eternal Agent" in Central

America from 1834 to 1852. This is a baseless charge. Chatfield did not create Central America's colonial mentality, her exaggerated localism, the ideological clash of 1826-29, the war, the economic and financial instability, the rivalry of states and municipalities, the opportunistic *caudillos*, the greed and selfishness of factions, the lack of national sentiment. On the contrary, Frederick Chatfield was a positive force during the life of the Republic in his collaboration with unionists like Morazán and Barrundia. For example, he recommended and drafted the tariff and customs legislation of 1837-38. His proposed loans and general bearing during the secessionist crisis of 1838 further confirm this impression; he thoroughly despised Carrera and the *serviles* and did everything possible to prevent the invasion of the Allied States. It was only *after* the events described above that he became a formidable foe of unionism in Central America because he feared that the re-establishment of a strong republic would endanger his country's territorial holdings in the area.

England welcomed the independence of Central America from Spain, and her subjects looked forward to developing the economic resources of that bountiful land. But complications soon arose in her diplomatic relations with the young Republic over a problem that had originated during the colonial period. Since the seventeenth century Englishmen had frequented the Caribbean coast of Central America as smugglers, defying the closed colonial trade system of Spain, and as woodcutters, very much interested in the mahogany and dyewood resources of the area. They allied themselves with the Mosquito Indians on the coast and eventually recognized a king of the Mosquitos (or Sambos, because Negroes from Jamaica mixed with the original Indians), whose domains extended from the coastal sections of modern Honduras to Costa Rica—the so-called Mosquito Shore. British subjects also visited the Bay Islands of Honduras and the coast of what is now British Honduras. Spaniards, of course, challenged these intrusions and the fiction of a Mosquito enclave on their flank.

The sheer power of the British navy, however, legalized this clandestine traffic on various occasions. By the Treaty of 1783 and a further convention of 1786. Spain gave the English woodcutting rights in the vicinity of Belize, providing England respected Spanish sovereignty in the area and did not establish settlements there. In addition, Great Britain agreed to keep her subjects from visiting the Bay Islands and the Mosquito Shore. Neither of these agreements was observed for long. A virtual state of war prevailed in the area as British subjects ventured beyond the treaty limits in search of the coveted wood. By 1821 the English-occupied territory around Belize was three to five times greater than authorized; only Spanish colonials in Yucatán had been able to contain the English advance along the Rio Hondo, the northern limits of the Belize concession.

With the achievement of independence, Central Americans argued that they had inherited their former king's sovereignty to Belize and that therefore Great Britain should regard the Republic as the grantor of the woodcutting concession. The English, and Frederick Chatfield in particular, refused to accept this "derivative" thesis, however well based it may have been in the legal tradition of Spain. Articulating the sentiments of Belizeans, Chatfield argued that the right of conquest, or effective occupation, should be the determining principle, a position that his country eventually adopted on the controversial Belize Question.

In April 1823 the territorial dispute made its first appearance when the national constituent assembly decreed the emancipation of slaves —enlightened legislation, perhaps, but infuriating to Belizeans, who assumed that this was a deliberate move to encourage the flight of their slaves. A belligerent commission of magistrates from Belize presented their case forcefully in Guatemala City, arousing a keen reaction among Central American nationalists. A diplomatic mission to London was unable to solve the fugitive slave issue or to gain recognition from the British government of Central America's rights to Belize. Instead, the contending parties in both Belize and Guatemala City resorted to economic warfare, levying discriminatory taxes on each other's products. As a result, Great Britain was unable to negotiate a commercial treaty with the Republic.

Yet the need for such a treaty was paramount to protect British interests at Belize and to offset the economic challenge of France and the United States in Central America. Chatfield's initial mission was that of minister plenipotentiary charged with negotiating a commercial treaty. During the last half of 1834 Chatfield labored constructively toward this end but was unable to prevent the territorial question from intruding into the negotiations. Nationalist sentiment in Guatemala demanded vindictive measures toward Belize. Rival British interests and the hostile attitude of Belizean magistrates further embarrassed the minister plenipotentiary. By the time the federal congress of 1835 opened its sessions, it appeared that Chatfield's mission was hopeless. Governor Gálvez of Guatemala, who led the strident nationalists, was demanding strong economic measures against Belize, and it seemed that he would have his way.[11] By then, moreover, the federal government had agreed to send John Galindo, of Irish ancestry, on a mission to the United States and Europe to secure support against the British position at Belize.[12]

Chatfield's most effective strategy against the Guatemalan nationalists, as it turned out, was the close alliance he nurtured with President Morazán and unionist liberals in general. He convinced them that a clash with Great Britain at this point in the Republic's development would be harmful; instead, they should work with him in tightening the mutual bonds that existed between British Belize and Central America. Because of this "Doctrine of Mutuality," Galvecistas were unable to pass vengeful measures against the British settlement in the federal congresses of 1835 and 1836—all of which made Chatfield realize that by supporting the Republic he would further England's position in Central America. That is why he offered to draw up a model for tariff and customs reforms, thereby winning the gratitude of President Morazán. His patient and constructive alliance with unionists yielded results, at least temporarily. The tariff of 1837 abolished the discriminatory levy against Belize, and the federal government agreed to repay the debts owed to British bondholders by setting aside a portion of the tobacco revenue that had been restored to the Republic.

But other factors gnawed away at the Chatfield-unionist bonds, until they snapped on March 4, 1839, when Morazán took the field against the Allied States. In late 1836 and early 1837 the territorial

[11] Ibid., pp. 89-119.
[12] William Joyce Griffith, "Juan Galindo, Central American Chauvinist," Hispanic American Historical Review, Vol. XL, No. 1 (February 1960), 25-52: Ian Graham, "Juan Galindo, Enthusiast," Estudios de Cultura Maya, III (Mexico, 1963), 11-35, presents a more favorable view.

controversy went beyond Belize to the Bay Islands and the Mosquito Shore, affecting now the interests of Honduras, Nicaragua, Costa Rica, and Guatemala. The bellicose Superintendent of Belize, Alexander Macdonald, was largely responsible for this by his determination to support Belizean expansion into new areas. All the states of the union clamored for action against the English, thus embarrassing Morazán's relations with the British representative. Although the two allies reasserted their respective positions toward the territories in dispute, they both realized that saving the union should have priority, and the alliance limped on for another two years.

While Macdonald was aggressively forwarding Belizean designs on the Bay Islands and Mosquito Shore, Chatfield was formulating the theoretical bases for British claims to those lands. Authorities in London opposed both courses of action until late 1838, when a Honduran commandant forbade any intercourse between Ruatán Island, the largest of the Bay Islands, and the British settlement at Belize; he also announced that Central America's colors would be raised on the island in the near future. As usual, Macdonald bellowed that he would resist such a move by force. Chatfield registered an official protest in a statesmanlike manner, but the Foreign Office, under Lord Palmerston, made it clear that England would not tolerate any flag-raising at Ruatán. In April 1839 an authorized British expedition occupied Ruatán Island, an action which reverberated in Central America for years. It would seem that the authorities in London had finally caught up with their agents in the field.

But Chatfield had no way of knowing that Lord Palmerston was about to take such a drastic step; he could only remember a long series of reprimands, indicating that Great Britain would not back up its claims along the lines that he had suggested. And he realized that Macdonald's actions were not authorized. During the crucial year of 1838, therefore, he tended to minimize the territorial questions and concentrated instead on helping the federal government solve its domestic difficulties. While the Allied States were threatening to invade El Salvador, he was negotiating a loan for the federal government, but unexpected difficulties arose at the last minute which made it impossible for him to give Morazán the money he needed to defend El Salvador. When Morazán levied a forced loan for this purpose, the frustrated British consul broke with his former ally. By this time, however, the Republic had been dissolved.[13]

The impact of the Ruatán crisis brought about a reversal in Chatfield's strategy and thinking. His former allies, the *Morazanistas*, pleaded for united action against British aggression, calculating that states' righters would now join them in a convention to form "a more perfect union," one that would command respect in foreign affairs. Unionists hoped, moreover, that the convention would favor resolutions to impose a boycott on British goods until Ruatán was abandoned and to seek the cooperation of all countries in the Western Hemisphere at a special inter-American gathering. To counter these measures, Chatfield established a working alliance with the *serviles* of Guatemala City. Because of their political ambitions —they had been out of power for a decade—the conservatives met all of Chatfield's terms, including the repeal of an article by which the previous Guatemalan government had reasserted its claim to Belize.[14]

To avoid notoriety, Chatfield urged his new allies to approach him indirectly on the matter of establishing a British protectorate of Central America. According to this plan Guatemala would ask the conservative government of Nicaragua to request a British guarantee of the peace in Central America. In the meantime, Chatfield would write to Palmerston encouraging him to accept this offer. On four separate occasions Chatfield asked the Foreign Office to intervene in the domestic affairs of Central America; in his last request, it was clear that he planned to use the British navy to support his allies in Guatemala and Nicaragua against the unionists.

By November 1839 the submissive Nicaraguan government did as it was told, sending a circular letter to all the states in behalf of a British guarantee of the peace in Central America. Chatfield's maneuver had the effect of bolstering morale among states' righters, who were fearful that the *Morazanistas* would succeed in establishing an effective union by appealing to the nationalistic sentiments of their countrymen. Conversely, the unionist states of El Salvador and Los Altos redoubled their efforts to rally the area against the English. In

---

[13] Rodríguez, *A Palmerstonian Diplomat*, pp. 149-209.
[14] *Ibid.*, p. 198.

the meantime, Lord Palmerston refused Chatfield's various requests for intervention, since they were obviously slanted to aid a particular group.

To bring the unionist enemy to his knees, Chatfield pursued an aggressive policy that set an important precedent for the future. First of all, he realized that he had to commit the British government to the use of naval power for political objectives and that this had to be done indirectly. One technique he developed to perfection was the presentation of reports that gave the impression that *Morazanistas* were not only Anglophobes but unscrupulous politicians who were seeking mere power; under no conditions was the Foreign Office to learn that there was an ideological basis for the instability of Central America. Moreover, he solicited the aid of every conceivable English interest that might apply pressure upon the Foreign Office to send their consul naval support. Finally, he raised certain claims against El Salvador in December 1839 that were deliberately calculated to frighten that unionist state and to assure himself the backing of the British navy.

Although Palmerston questioned many of the claims presented by his consul and refused to accept Chatfield's premises on forced loans, he nevertheless assigned British squadrons in the Pacific and Atlantic to collect those claims that *Chatfield* judged to be fair ones.[15] It was this authorization of August 1840 that served as the basis for the British blockades of 1842 and 1844, as well as other naval actions of the late forties and early fifties. England was thus committed to an imperialistic position in Central America without her knowing it, all the while assuming that Chatfield was only protecting the lives and property of Englishmen. Central Americans, on the other hand, were aware of Chatfield's political objectives all along, from the manner in which he dropped or resurrected claims as conditions dictated. It is not surprising, therefore, that Central Americans developed an aversion to foreign intervention and have always been suspicious of its objectives.

The State of Los Altos was also a thorn in Chatfield's side. In late January 1840 Rafael Carrera invaded the highlands and destroyed that government, dealing a severe blow to the unionist movement.

[15] *Ibid.*, pp. 214-18.

When, in December of the previous year, Chatfield and the *serviles* had decided upon this action, they fully realized that it would lead to a military showdown with General Morazán. Since they had received a key shipment of arms, as well as Chatfield's assurance that he could get more from Belize, the *serviles* were willing to gamble that they could defeat the Salvadorean forces under Morazán. And their strategy bore fruit; Morazán's partisans were routed in the famous battle of Guatemala City on March 18-19, 1840, forcing the erstwhile President and his allies into exile. The first unionist movement since the fall of the Republic had failed, and Frederick Chatfield played a major role in this failure by bolstering the morale of his states' rights allies. In the process, he set important precedents for the future.

Divided We Fall (1842-1852)

Despite the nationalistic overtones of the Ruatán crisis, the will for power dominated the minds of states' righters of both the liberal and conservative variety. Regardless of the rationale they developed in refusing to unite with *Morazanistas* against the common enemy, the fact still remains that they collaborated unabashedly with the agent whose country had occupied Ruatán. If they had been as sincerely interested in establishing a confederation as they claimed to be, then it is reasonable to assume that a genuine effort would have been made to hold a states' rights convention. That this did not take place in the two years following the rout of General Morazán underscored their real motive for resisting unionism: the lust for power in their separate states. This generalization is further buttressed by the record of unionism during the years 1842 to 1852, which coincides with Chatfield's return to Central America after a two-year leave of absence.

Once Chatfield had left the scene of victory in the fall of 1840, Superintendent Macdonald of Belize and the admiral of the Atlantic squadron assumed responsibility for collecting the claims that the consul had raised against El Salvador, though now all five states were made proportionally responsible for those debts. For one reason or another, no payment was made on them. In the meantime, Macdonald continued his aggressive ways in advancing the claims of the puppet Mosquito king, a hopeless alcoholic who blindly acquiesced to the forceful blandishments of his English master. In early 1840, for example, Macdonald imposed upon him a special advisory commission, made up of himself and other Belizean officials, to help run the Mosquito Shore, a project that Chatfield sanctioned and later persuaded Palmerston to accept. But Lord John Russell, in charge of the Colonial Office, rejected the scheme precisely because it implied a British protectorate of the Mosquito Shore.

Unwilling to submit to his superior's decision, Colonel Macdonald created a crisis in August 1841 that eventually forced Great Britain's hand on the troublesome Mosquito Question. He kidnapped the Nicaraguan commandant at the port of San Juan de Nicaragua (now San Juan del Norte) while on a tour of the Mosquito Shore, laying claim to Boca del Toro (now called Bocas del Toro)—to which Nueva Granada (Colombia) also had a claim—and to the Great Corn Island. Realizing that the abduction of Manuel Quijano would result in a sharp reprimand from London, the aggressive Macdonald, copying a page from Chatfield's mode of operation, insisted upon Central America's prompt payment of the old 1839 claims while at the same time picturing his adversaries as prototypes of the "Black Legend," irresponsible Latins unwilling to pay their bills to English creditors. When Central Americans reacted strongly to Quijano's abduction, refusing to deal with Macdonald under any conditions and insisting that Great Britain punish him and issue orders to all subalterns to refrain from further unauthorized action, British pride did the rest—the blockade of 1842 and England's acceptance of protectorate of the Mosquito Shore in late 1843, a policy she had refused to condone since 1837.[16]

Central American unionism was revived as a result of Macdonald's intemperate action at San Juan de Nicaragua. This time it was the states' righters who realized the folly of disunion, and in 1842 the three center states signed the *Pacto de Chinandega*, which embodied defensive measures of the type the *Morazanistas* had urged three years earlier in connection with Ruatán. Even Rafael Carrera reacted violently to the kidnapping of Quijano, and the *serviles* themselves came to favor action against the English.

[16] *Ibid.*, pp. 244-46.

Chatfield returned to the Central American battleground in mid-1842. But the English agent—he now sported the rank of consul-general—was not the only key figure who returned to Central America during this crisis; General Francisco Morazán heeded the call made by Nicaragua and returned to his native land to unite it against the common enemy. His presence, however, reawakened the apprehensions of states' righters, and once again their hunger for power defeated the unionist effort. They turned on Morazán, and on September 15, 1842, he was shot by a Costa Rican firing squad. With Morazán out of the way, the states' righters elected to form a confederation based on the *Pacto de Chinandega*. Headed by the Nicaraguan conservative Fruto Chamorro, the Confederation of Central America existed feebly from 1844 to only 1845, unable to command the allegiance of squabbling *caudillos* or to win the recognition of European powers. Unionism of a conservative variety proved unequal to the task.

In this second unionist revival Frederick Chatfield once again disrupted the movement for Central American unity. He did this by dividing the states' righters, offering them a confederation project to be controlled by the Guatemalan *serviles*, the "Guatemalan Confederation," as a substitute for the Chinandega plan of 1842. The difference between these two movements—and it must be realized that the *Morazanistas* represented a third variety—was significant. Chatfield wanted a general government whose capital would always be Guatemala City, one that would not raise embarrassing issues concerning England's territorial program in Central America. In attempting to implement this rival confederation, Chatfield persuaded his allies in Guatemala City to reject the Chinandega plan. He applied pressure on Honduras, the weakest link in the Chinandega chain, by threatening to revive a special claim against the government of Francisco Ferrera and raised a series of claims against Nicaragua in order to quiet her protests concerning the Mosquito Shore. When Nicaragua refused to acquiesce, Chatfield prepared the Foreign Office for a second blockade in 1844, which brought the recalcitrant state to her knees. It was in response to this second blockade that the Confederation of Central America was formed in 1844 and the

mission of Francisco Castellón was sent to Europe to demand—un·
successfully—Chatfield's recall. For various reasons, among which the
element of English pride again figured prominently, Lord Aberdeen,
who headed the Foreign Office at that time, refused to consider
Castellón's demands or even recognize the Confederation he represented. Other European powers considered it wise not to challenge
England at this time.

The failure of the Castellón mission of 1845 had important repercussions in Central America. It now became clear to everyone that
Chatfield commanded the support of his home authorities. This
awareness contributed to the revived popularity of *Morazanistas*; a
strong republic, they argued, was the only solution to Chatfield's constant meddling in Central American affairs. Thus, in 1846 at Sonsonate, El Salvador, and in 1847 at Nacaome, Honduras, unionists
pleaded with states' righters to forget their past dissensions and to
unite against the British. Although many of the governments sent
delegates to these conventions because popular opinion in their
states required it, they had no genuine intentions of supporting a
strong union movement.

In meeting this third unionist revival, Chatfield sharpened some
of his old tools, the "Guatemalan Confederation" in particular. He
felt that this time the *Morazanistas* might succeed, especially if they
could attract the support of the United States. In fact, since mid-1846
Chatfield had been obsessed with the notion that the United States,
after terminating its war with Mexico, would spring next to Central
America. To thwart the Sonsonate and Nacaome meetings, therefore, he revived the "Guatemalan Confederation" scheme. He urged
Guatemala to declare her independence in 1847; next, he negotiated
a trade treaty with the new nation along the lines of his 1834 instructions, though slightly more generous; finally, he got Costa Rica
to sign an "act of accession" to the treaty. If he could have gotten the
other three states to do likewise, he would have implemented his
plan: Guatemala City, in effect, would have been the recognized capital of Central America, enjoying trade relations with Great Britain
that would be available to all other states recognizing her superior
position. Needless to say, neither Guatemala nor Costa Rica joined

their sisters at Nacaome in the fall of 1847, and Chatfield, as well as his agents in the center states, did his best to encourage the defection of the state governments meeting in Honduras.

On January 1, 1848, a combined British-Mosquito force occupied San Juan de Nicaragua, renaming it Greytown. This event, like Macdonald's Quijano venture earlier in the decade, rallied Central Americans momentarily and strengthened the hand of unionist liberals. More importantly, it made the United States realize that Great Britain was determined to monopolize any interoceanic passegeway that might be constructed through Central America; to be sure, Chatfield had no intentions of permitting any other country to command this important route, judging from the many suggestions he was making to Lord Palmerston. The Foreign Office, moreover, was not unmindful of Chatfield's recommendations, even to the point of secretly surveying the Gulf of Fonseca for the best commanding position on the Pacific side of the projected canal route. Palmerston's announcement of Mosquito limits in 1847, plus the advanced warning that the king of the Mosquitos would occupy San Juan on the first of the year, confirmed the American suspicion that England intended to dominate the passageway through Central America. Heeding American interest in the Pacific Coast—the Oregon Territory and subsequently the discovery of gold in California—the United States decided to challenge England in Central America. This in turn prompted Lord Palmerston to encourage Chatfield to block North American maneuvers there, a support he grudgingly qualified because of a strong current of English opinion that opposed an aggressive Mosquito policy.

Desperately seeking an effective counterpoise to Chatfield, unionist liberals in Nicaragua placed themselves under the protection of the United States, offering the Northern republic, or any corporation it favored, exclusive rights to a passageway across their country—the Elijah Hise-Buenaventura Selva Convention of June 1849. To preserve her own claims to the Mosquito Shore south of the San Juan River, Nueva Granada negotiated a treaty with Benjamin Bidlack, ratified by the U.S. Senate on June 3, 1848, which gave the United States transit rights across the Isthmus of Panama in return for a guarantee of the neutrality of that area. Moreover, Ephraim George

Squier, who replaced Hise in mid-1849, actively countered Chatfield's moves by negotiating treaties with both Nicaragua and Honduras. The latter state, insulted by the tactics of a British naval commander at Trujillo and mindful of the persistent rumor that Chatfield was about to occupy the strategic island of Tigre in the Gulf of Fonseca, temporarily ceded Tigre Island to Squier.

On October 16, 1849, Frederick Chatfield, accompanied by a British naval force, occupied Tigre Island, raised his country's colors there, and assigned a superintendent to manage the island. Without question this was an unauthorized and premeditated action, not just a spontaneous reaction to Squier's agreement with Honduras. In fact, Chatfield first proposed this action to Palmerston in January, 1847, when he asked the Foreign Office to survey the Gulf of Fonseca. On his own initiative he had tried to get Englishmen to buy property on the mainland near the strategic base, also proposing the use of claims against both El Salvador and Honduras to advance this political objective. Faced with a hostile opposition in London, Lord Palmerston could not condone this aggressive suggestion. After receiving Palmerston's last refusal on this subject, Chatfield took matters into his own hands, forcing the celebrated crisis between Great Britain and the United States that was temporarily solved by the Clayton-Bulwer Treaty of April 19, 1850.[17]

The forceful occupation of Tigre Island united the center states almost overnight. Although the Nacaome pact had not produced a general government after the Greytown incident of 1848, Chatfield's maneuver did. In November 1849 the center states met in León, Nicaragua, to sign a new pact that envisioned a government to be called the National Representation (*Representación Nacional*), which was born in January 1851, the third general government of Central America. It had no better luck than its conservative counter-part of 1844-45. Of course, Chatfield did his best to thwart the unionists at León, while Squier worked just as assiduously to promote union in Central America. In the process the two English-speaking adversaries launched an ideological campaign that aroused and inspired their followers. Squier, as the champion of the "Western Hemisphere Idea"—Professor Arthur P. Whitaker's name for it—in-

[17] *Ibid.*, pp. 281-306.

sisted that the Americas were for Americans, reserved for the experiment in republicanism. From Costa Rica the Englishman countered by attacking the "American System" as isolationist, underscoring the incompatibility of race-conscious North Americans and mixed-blood Latin Americans. Instead, he argued, the center states should follow the wise example of Guatemala and Costa Rica. Since Palmerston had vetoed Costa Rica's "act of accession," preferring to recognize her as an independent country, Chatfield's strategy had to change accordingly. He would now try to commit the center states to a declaration of their independence, in this way undermining the *Pacto de León*.

After Great Britain abandoned Tigre Island to satisfy the United States, Chatfield went on consolidating his nation's position in Central America and bolstering the morale of faltering allies in Guatemala and Costa Rica. He successfully undermined the mission sent to Costa Rica by adherents of the Leonese pact, bribing the envoy Felipe Jáuregui to revolutionize Honduras and declare her independence in conjunction with General Santos Guardiola. In return, Chatfield promised to drop a long-standing claim against Honduras in which Jáuregui was a principal; this same claim had been used earlier to dissociate Honduras from the Confederation of 1844-45. The Jáuregui-Guardiola coup was not successful, though General Guardiola later headed the conservative government of Honduras. In Costa Rica, Chatfield had no trouble maintaining the alliance when a frightened Juan José Mora pleaded for the protection of the British against the unionists.

From Costa Rica, Chatfield traveled to Greytown and made many precedent-establishing innovations, a number of which England subsequently adopted: the assignment of warships to protect the king of the Mosquitos from a Nicaraguan uprising, the enlistment of a modern police force, the erection of a municipal body at Greytown, and so forth. Furthermore, the governor and naval authorities in Jamaica gave their blessings to Chatfield's measures. And in Belize and the Bay Islands the indefatigable agent urged colonists to petition the home government for colonial status. In 1852 the Bay Islands were made a crown colony, as was Belize after another decade. Back in Guatemala, the Englishman had to reassert his control over his erstwhile allies, the *serviles*, who had given ground to the unionists on some points. General Rafael Carrera, however, had successfully resisted an invasion of Guatemala by the Anglophobes of the center states.

Although Palmerston had yielded to conciliatory voices in England, thus making possible the negotiations between John Clayton and Henry Bulwer, he tacitly supported his aggressive underling by providing the naval power needed to collect the various claims Chatfield had raised to achieve political objectives—it should be noted that Chatfield no longer bothered to conceal his political machinations from Palmerston. To bring down the troublesome state of El Salvador, headed by Doroteo Vasconcelos, one of the leading unionist liberals of the day, Chatfield instigated the blockade of the winter 1850-51. In response to this maneuver the *Representación Nacional* (RN) was inaugurated in January 1851 and insisted upon the lifting of the blockade. At the same time, because Chatfield would not recognize the general government, the RN withdrew his exequatur. According to the RN, Great Britain no longer had a representative in Central America. Determined to end the "Eternal Agent's" control over the *serviles*, an expeditionary force sanctioned by the RN invaded Guatemala. At the Battle of Arada, on February 2, 1851, Carrera again defeated the unionist adversary. For all practical purposes this ended the third unionist movement in Central America, though the Honduran government of José Trinidad Cabañas fought a rearguard action until 1854.

The Fire of Prometheus (1851-1865)

According to the Clayton-Bulwer Treaty of April 19, 1850, Great Britain and the United States agreed that neither party would seek exclusive control of a transit route through the Middle American land mass, nor fortify, colonize, or settle in Central America in such a way as to interfere with the projected canal route. They would jointly support the Atlantic and Pacific Steam Navigation Company, one of whose directors was Cornelius Vanderbilt, in its efforts to construct a transit route through Nicaragua. There were to be free ports at the termini of this passageway. Conscientiously, the Foreign Office encouraged British bankers to welcome Vanderbilt's request for financial support, and Lord Palmerston promised the company that the authorities at Greytown would not interfere in any way with their work. He therefore vetoed Chatfield's tariff schedule and made Greytown a free port. However commendable, this measure left the Mosquito authorities at the port without revenues to garrison Greytown. To offset this loss of revenue, the Mosquito officials implemented Chatfield's suggestion concerning the establishment of a municipality, and the town fathers of Greytown then proceeded to levy minor port charges.

On November 21, 1851, the captain of the *Prometheus*, one of Vanderbilt's ships carrying passengers to and from New York, refused to pay the port charges. The irascible "Commodore," who happened to be present on this occasion, insisted vehemently that he would not pay charges that violated both the Clayton-Bulwer Treaty and the promises Palmerston had made to his company. The upshot of this incident was that Mosquito authorities appealed to the British warship, the *Express*, to enforce their regulations. When the *Express* fired over the *Prometheus*, Vanderbilt paid his bill under protest. The treaty had been put to its first test, and there followed a decade of ill feeling between the United States and Great Britain.

The details of that troublesome decade of Anglo-American diplomacy need not concern us here.[18] The *Prometheus* incident drew fire from the American public and strengthened the hand of Palmerston's enemies in England, who insisted that "Old Pam's" gunboat diplomacy had harmed British interests all over the world. Lord Palmerston resigned as foreign secretary in late December 1851, and Chatfield was recalled a few weeks later, thus ending Great Britain's aggressive policy in Central America. Determined to liquidate all traces of its former policy, the Foreign Office sought to extricate itself from the Mosquito protectorate with honor—by the Webster-Crampton Agreement of 1852, among others—and from the Bay Islands by the Dallas-Clarendon Convention of 1856, neither of which agreements, unfortunately, was implemented, due to Central American, English, and North American opposition in the area as

<hr/>

[18] Mario Rodríguez, "The *Prometheus* and the Clayton-Bulwer Treaty," *Journal of Modern History*, XXXVI (September 1964), 260-78, provides details of these relations.

well as the saber-rattling tactics of U.S. politicians. Thus, in 1859 and 1860 Charles Wyke, Chatfield's successor, negotiated separate treaties with Honduras, Nicaragua, and Guatemala settling their differences with Great Britain, at least for the time being.

Hoping that his recall was only temporary and that Great Britain would again resume its aggressive stance in Central America, Mr. Chatfield left the area in May 1852. Though the blockade of 1850-51 had failed to destroy Doroteo Vasconcelos, the naval action of the following winter finished the job. The pesky unionist government of El Salvador fell from power, and Francisco Dueñas, a former unionist liberal, organized a government that danced to the English fiddler's tune. With three states under his control, Chatfield was in his strongest position just when his recall orders reached Guatemala City.

Although he never returned to Central America, Chatfield's influence lingered on through the actions of Manuel Francisco Pavón, his ex-secretary and one of the leading *serviles* of Guatemala. Until his death in 1855 Pavón had much to say in General Carrera's government; he was particularly interested in negotiating a treaty with England to prevent Belize from falling into the hands of the United States, a policy his old friend in London had suggested to him. Undoubtedly this explains why Charles Wyke was able to negotiate the 1859 treaty concerning the boundary limits of British Honduras.[19] Moreover, Chatfield's divide-and-conquer tactics continued to bear fruit in Central America, only now it was Rafael Carrera who urged the neighboring states to set up republics to undermine the unionist movement. After the Battle of Arada the *serviles* felt secure enough to enact a constitution of their liking, re-establishing the corporate institutions of the colonial period and preserving power in their hands. By the Consultative Act of 1851 Rafael Carrera became absolute master of Guatemala; in 1854 his admiring supporters declared him president for life. By that time the talented conservative Fruto Chamorro was leading Nicaragua along the same path to "Liberty, Order, and Work" for the good of the nation.

[19] Wayne M. Clegern, "New Light on the Belize Dispute," *The American Journal of International Law*, LII (April 1958), 280-97, is excellent on this subject.

After the defeat at Arada in February 1851 the *Representación Nacional* tried vainly to rally its supporters. Dueñas of El Salvador would not listen. Chamorro of Nicaragua had his eyes set on the independence of his state. Only Honduras remained faithful; the RN therefore moved to Tegucigalpa in October 1852, where unionists drew up the *Estatuto*, a provisional constitution, hoping that all Central Americans, now that Chatfield had left, would gather together at a national constituent assembly.

But the lust for power again prevailed. Dueñas refused to send his delegates from El Salvador on March 24, 1853. Chamorro followed suit on April 30, 1853, and, of course, the Guatemalan government encouraged these defections. Elected to the presidency of Honduras in March 1852, General José Trinidad Cabañas, a *Morazanista* of long standing, pleaded with his neighbors of the center to keep the cause of union uppermost in their minds. When peaceful suggestions failed, Cabañas invaded Guatemala in July 1853, at the same time making threatening gestures at El Salvador. On July 6, 1853, General Vicente Cerna, Carrera's right-hand man, defeated Cabañas and thus emboldened conservatives throughout Central America. By 1854 Rafael Carrera, the ex-muleteer, was not only the perpetual president of Guatemala but thenceforth the undisputed master of Central America for the next 11 years.

But unionist liberals had a disturbing way of resurging to the fore. Thoroughly frustrated by Carrera's power, they sought aid from the outside. In June 1855 William Walker and 58 companions landed in Nicaragua, muddying Central American waters that were already far from potable. It is difficult to say what motivated this "grey-eyed" man of destiny; perhaps the famous Tennessean did not know himself. One thing is sure, he had an uncanny ability for arousing everyone's opposition—the unionist liberals who had called for his support, the conservatives who suspected his personal ambitions and possible connection with the United States government, and Cornelius Vanderbilt, who resented his countryman's interference with the transit company. The combined forces of his various enemies brought down this diminutive President of Nicaragua in 1857; three years later, while trying to return to Central America, he fell before a Honduran firing squad. The conservative governments of Central

America hailed the victory of the "National Army of Liberation" under President Juan José Mora of Costa Rica as if somehow it atoned for their otherwise shabby record against foreign foes. With the spirit of euphoria that attended the downfall of William Walker, it almost seemed that this time—the fourth, according to our count—unionism might triumph in Central America. Mora of Costa Rica and Tomás Martínez of Nicaragua, both conservatives, negotiated a territorial settlement of the troublesome Guanacaste dispute in 1858, and unionist liberals, like Gerardo Barrios of El Salvador and Máximo Jérez of Nicaragua, began to work closely with conservative leaders. It all added up to the impression that a new era of national cooperation was in the offing. Elected to the presidency of his country in 1860, Gerardo Barrios, who had been instrumental in revolutionizing the Nicaragua of Fruto Chamorro in 1853, gave Carrera reason to believe that he would be a friendly ally. Barrios proposed a convention in 1862 to form a general government of the three center states; his friend Jérez, in the meantime, had persuaded President Martínez of Nicaragua to join the scheme.

In keeping with his long record as a *Morazanista*, Gerardo Barrios envisioned a strong republic of the "center," consisting of two evenly matched districts in each of the three states, subordinate to the national government. But Martínez of Nicaragua apparently was not serious about the project; in what was almost a revival of the "Guatemalan Confederation" scheme of Mr. Chatfield, he suggested that Guatemala be included in the new government and that Rafael Carrera be named provisional president. Gerardo Barrios rejected the proposals outright, of course, and Carrera likewise disappoved, or so it is said. Yet Carrera must have had more than a passing interest in Martínez' recommendations. Guatemala renewed her war with El Salvador in 1863, ousting Barrios from power and imposing Francisco Dueñas on the Salvadoreans. The unionist government of Honduras also fell, and Carrera set up José María Medina to mind the store there.

From his exile in Costa Rica the ex-Salvadorean President prepared for a comeback. But on his way through Nicaragua, Barrios was detained by President Martínez who turned him over to the Dueñas government. After a rigged trial, Gerardo Barrios fell before a firing squad on August 29, 1865. His last will and testament is a graphic reminder of the intense unionist fervor that had inspired *Morazanistas* since the downfall of the Republic—a movement always outnumbered and never able to contend with the swaggering *caudillos* spawned by the anarchy of that ideological struggle. The craze for power was simply too strong in the minds of Central America's conservatives, states' rights liberals, and military opportunists to permit the restoration of the Republic.

By 1865 Carrera and his conservative puppets were in complete control of the situation in all five countries of Central America. Perhaps it was poetic justice that on April 14th of that year Guatemala's lifetime President breathed his last, an enigmatic figure whose name still arouses controversy in his native country. The representatives of the highlands in the present National Constituent Assembly of Guatemala angrily rejected any consideration of the proposal to erect a monument to Carrera on the centennial of his death.

General Vicente Cerna, Carrera's heir apparent, continued the system of government his predecessor had established—the ironclad dictatorship of the "families," the dictator's bureaucracy, and the Church, whose power and properties had long since been restored by Carrera.

The deaths of Gerardo Barrios and Rafael Carrera marked the end of Central America's formative years, a violent period of ideological struggles and unadorned selfishness that the colonial past had almost institutionalized. Because of the machinations of aggressive British agents, the power of the world's leading nation worked against unionism and the establishment of liberal institutions; the traditional elements and centrifugal forces in the Central American environment did the rest. It remained to be seen, however, whether or not the victory of the conservatives and states' righters could survive the death of their champion.

THREE

THE NEW LIBERALISM

1871-1941

This [horsewhip] is the constitution I govern by.[1]
Justo Rufino Barrios

In the 1870s Central Americans marched into the modern world under the leadership of vigorous men who took cognizance of historical fact and based their actions on the positivistic writings of the day. Seeking power for its own sake and for the opportunity it gave them to fashion stable and prosperous governments, these new liberals worshipped economic progress. They were determined to extract the maximum benefit from the nation's resources through a centralized and benevolent government that dispensed favors freely to both foreign and domestic entrepreneurs. Traditional values and institutions that hampered the nation's material welfare were discarded irretrievably, and the new leaders paid only lip service to constitutionalism as a sop for the romantics in their midst. Power was for those who understood what was best for the nation.

By ignoring the democratic means that is perhaps the most basic tenet of liberalism, these new liberals in fact abandoned their earlier faith. Not surprisingly, conservatives welcomed this change of heart, as well as the program of social order and economic development,

[1] Paul Burgess, *Justo Rufino Barrios: A Biography* (Dorrance and Co., Philadelphia, 1926), p. 134.

thus blurring the lines between the two historic rivals. The *person-alista* age was upon Central America, and elections degenerated into a periodic fight for spoils of office.

Instability was a constant factor in the Central American scene, much to the annoyance of foreigners. Crass opportunism reigned everywhere. States developed an increasing awareness of the regional balance-of-power complex, and unionism distracted the best minds, encouraging the historic pattern of intervention in each other's affairs. Alarmed by the constant turbulence, foreign powers threatened to defend their interests by force if need be, and the onerous task of guaranteeing the peace in Central America fell upon the shoulders of the United States, the protector of the Canal Zone. North American intervention—gunboat diplomacy, the use of marines, and fiscal controls—aroused the spirited enmity of liberals and unionists, especially since the conservatives benefited from it. Yet the unionist movement faltered as it had before and finally gave way, in the depression years, to national *caudillos* who mastered the process of *continuismo*.

"Peace, Education, and Material Prosperity"

This slogan underscored the changed emphasis of the liberalism which broke upon the Central American stage in the "revolution of 1871," toppling from power the conservatives of Guatemala, El Salvador, Honduras, and Costa Rica. The lone survivor was Nicaragua, where Granada's "families" ruled for more than three decades, until 1893 to be exact. Even there, however, the conservatives sympathized with the objectives of their liberal neighbors.

An elderly general, Miguel García Granados, headed the Guatemalan revolution of 1871. Having befriended Carrera in the 1830s, this Spanish-born liberal accommodated himself to the rule of the conservatives and led what little opposition was permitted during the regimes of Carrera and Vicente Cerna. Forced into exile after Cerna's bald attempt to prolong his rule, García Granados outfitted a revolutionary army in Mexico and joined forces with the popular rebel from the highlands of Guatemala, Justo Rufino Barrios. On June 30, 1871, the revolutionaries entered Guatemala City in triumph, and the old general took over the provisional government, assigning

Barrio, who was only in his mid-thirties, to the military district of Los Altos.

In temperament and manner of action, García Granados and Barrios illustrated graphically the dichotomy of the liberal movement. Because of his personality, his ties with the *serviles*, and his firm convictions about constitutional government, García Granados hoped for a peaceful transition to liberal institutions and was disposed to compromise with his former adversaries. He wanted to prepare the nation gradually for effective representative government by establishing schools, protecting the rights of the individual, and implementing the rule of law. Envisioning a modern and scientifically trained army, for example, he founded the *Escuela Politécnica* in the first years of the revolution. Yet his statesmanlike ways and spirit of compromise did not placate the extreme conservatives, who plotted incessantly to overthrow the regime. Resistance was especially fierce among the devout Catholics of eastern Guatemala, the traditional stronghold of clericalism that had produced Rafael Carrera. As a result, García Granados spent his rule on the battlefield, and his constructive projects were held in abeyance.

Justo Rufino Barrios was of a different mold, and it was he who dominated the revolution from its inception with his actions and counsels during the absence of García Granados on the battlefield. By June 1873 he had replaced García Granados as president of Guatemala and the old General accepted the inevitable. Also a liberal, educated in law at the University of San Carlos, the "Giant of Los Altos" was a proud *chivo* (goat) who resented the discriminatory practices of the well-to-do families in Guatemala City. On his plantation, which straddled the Mexican-Guatemalan border, Barrios had given evidence of business acumen, making his fortune by experimenting with various crops, coffee in particular. Perhaps it was his love for the highlands and his determination to right the wrongs inflicted upon Los Altos by Guatemala City interests, much in the vein of the earlier *provincianos*, that led Barrios to begin his career as a rebel. It should be noted that among his reforms were a special appellate court for Los Altos—a reform the highlanders had wanted since the late 1830s—an Indian institute for Quezaltenango, a western university, and a western bank.

But Barrios was more than a sectionalist; he was a confirmed Guatemalan nationalist. His government would serve and promote all sections of the country, not just Guatemala City. His various projects to stimulate the nation's economic body included railroads to the Pacific ports of San José and Champerico from Guatemala City and Retalhuleu respectively; roads to his beloved highlands, especially Quezaltenango; colonization and communication facilities for the interior area around Cobán; and a railroad outlet to the Atlantic coast, with an ambitious scheme for the development of the port of Livingston. And when he had begun to forge a nation, his vision encompassed another loyalty—Central Americanism.[2]

A pragmatist and brutal realist who knew the lessons of Central American history well, Justo Rufino Barrios regarded the gradualist approach of his senior as suicidal for liberalism. Appeasing the enemy was sheer nonsense, for there was nothing in Guatemala's past to indicate that the conservative would calmly relinquish control over the minds of the credulous masses. The conservative understood and respected the horsewhip; that was the only way to discourage the reactionary Church from inciting rebellion in eastern Guatemala. To quash this resistance once and for all, he expelled the Jesuit order and stripped the Church of all its power and possessions, an attractive program that helped to finance his various projects. Thus, Barrios had brought peace to eastern Guatemala by the end of 1873, and within seven years his deliberate anticlericalism had reduced the once-powerful Guatemalan Church to a meek tool of the state as punishment for its open support of the *serviles* in the long struggle against the *Morazanistas*.[3] The parallels with Mexican history are striking; Barrios' results were equally permanent.

To secure the revolution, Barrios also found it expedient to intervene in neighboring states; in fact, he took Carrera's place as president-maker of Central America. In July 1871 Guatemala recognized the spoiler of Costa Rica's families, General Tomás Guardia. Since El Salvador was safe—the liberal revolution of April 1871 had put Santiago González in control there—Barrios' immediate problem was the conservative Honduran government of José María Medina, Carrera's puppet, which was permitting Guatemalan exiles to recoup their forces on its territory. Medina fell in 1872, and Celeo Arias, a liberal of strong convictions, took his place. Thus did Barrios starve the revolt of eastern Guatemala.

The pattern of intervention in Honduras—a defense measure with an ideological base—was repeated, but not always in so clear-cut a fashion; other motives often cluttered the picture and contributed to regional anarchy. After Medina's defeat, and considering the liberal line-up in all the states except Nicaragua, it seemed that liberalism would now have a chance to breathe. But the advantage was short-lived. Conservative exiles flocked to Nicaragua and to Costa Rica, where Guardia, for reasons of his own, chose to give them asylum and permitted Enrique Palacios, a Guatemalan, to outfit a liberating expedition. Forewarned, the liberals stopped Palacios' invasion of Honduras, and subsequently compelled Nicaragua to sign a defensive alliance against Costa Rica.

At this point the liberals fell to quarreling, torn apart by personal ambition and differences in their alleged national objectives. González, who despised Arias of Honduras, wanted him replaced by Ponciano Leíva, and Barrios foolishly accepted the proposal. Then, Leíva and González, who seemed to be leading their governments toward conservatism, aroused Barrios' suspicions. The result, with the details eliminated, was the war of 1876 between El Salvador and Guatemala—a defeat for the challenging liberal adversaries. Barrios then selected Rafael Zaldívar and Marco Aurelio Soto to head the governments of El Salvador and Honduras respectively. Soto, a sincere liberal who had served as a minister in Barrios' government, brought long-needed reforms to Honduras and governed well. Barrios, however, forced him to resign in 1883 when he learned that Soto had advocated Central American union without the services of Guatemala's leader. Zaldívar too challenged the "Giant of Los Altos" two years later. In short, disunity among liberal leaders was an important factor in the strife of those years.

Whether by coincidence or design, Barrios' reform program bore the marks of positivism as outlined by Auguste Comte, the French sociologist. The influence may have come from the north as a result of the contacts of a Mexican educator, Gabino Barreda, with Comte from 1849 to 1851. Or it may have reached Central America independently; *El Progreso*, a Salvadorean periodical edited by José Francisco Barrundia, was discussing the new ideas in considerable detail during the early 1850's. Whatever the source, Guatemalan intellectuals like Manuel Antonio Herrera and Valero Pujol, to name only a few of them, were advocates of positivism, and they helped to guide Barrios' educational reforms.[4]

The educational decrees of 1875 and 1879 established a secular curriculum in the schools of Guatemala that proscribed the theological and metaphysical approach to knowledge and treated students as moral and social entities. University reforms followed the same positivistic orientation. Just as Porfirio Díaz had done in Mexico, Barrios deliberately trained a generation of *científicos* to implement his ambitious developmental program for Guatemala. In every respect his schools were modern institutions under the strict control of the minister of education and subsidized by the government.

To undertake the manifold responsibilities of a modern state, government had to be scientific and pragmatic. According to Barrios, a unitary republic best suited the needs of his country. The decree-laws of the 1870s, as well as the constitution of 1879, implemented the highlander's concept of government: a modern dictatorship adorned with constitutional trappings. Both the legislature and the judiciary were mere appendages of executive power. And Article 39 of the constitution, which gave the president, working with his council of ministers, the right to declare martial law, made a mockery of individual guarantees. Ministers were appointed by him and responsible to him alone. Barrios also selected the *jefes políticos* who controlled the minutest detail of provincial life; even the municipalities, which in theory had extensive authority and followed democratic procedures, were closely supervised by agents of the executive power. Justo Rufino Barrios was the state; no contemporaries ever doubted that.

[4] Ernesto Chinchilla Aguilar, *El positivismo y la reforma en Guatemala* (Guatemala, 1961), pp. 3-11, offers a brief analysis. Copies of *El Progreso* are in the Bancroft Library of the University of California in Berkeley.

The saving feature of Barrios' government—though the same cannot be said of subsequent Guatemalan administrations—was its efficiency and modernity. It called for a census in 1880, reorganized the post office and linked it to the Universal Postal Union, made vaccination compulsory, established a modern police force, instituted a double-entry procedure of bookkeeping, gathered *jefes políticos* annually to discuss administrative reforms and development projects, sponsored Central Americanism, as well as nationalism, by the publication of historical works, held expositions of Indian relics, preventing anyone from taking them out of the country, encouraged the use of the latest technical inventions from abroad, took over control of cemeteries and the registry of vital statistics, passed copyright laws, insisted upon civil marriages, and even supervised the medical inspection of prostitutes.

Barrios also felt that the modern state should provide the basic facilities of the economy. During the decade and a half of his rule Guatemala built a cartroad system that united the country, constructed the Guatemala City-San José railroad and the 30-mile stretch from Retalhuleu to Champerico, negotiated a contract to open up the Cobán area via the Polichic River, made plans to connect her railroads with the Mexican Southern Railway, sponsored an ambitious scheme to link Guatemala City with the Atlantic—a railroad project financed by bonds that Guatemalans of a certain earning capacity had to purchase on the installment plan—put up bridges, established telegraphy and telephone facilities, subsidized steamship operations, and passed enlightened tariff legislation to promote commerce with the outside world.

As Barrios boasted before his re-election in 1880, his government's main objective was material progress. In modern parlance, the "Great Reformer" dedicated himself to "sowing" the economy. He encouraged capitalists to exploit the mineral and wood resources of Guatemala, instructed *jefes políticos* to form nurseries of coffee trees and to produce at least 1,000 pounds of coffee annually in their respective provinces, protected coffee planters and assured them of adequate labor at harvest time, sponsored banana plantations on the north coast to capitalize upon the demand for bananas in the United States, gave free land to those persons who set up plantations of rubber, cocoa, and sarsaparilla, stimulated the cattle industry in various sections of the country, helped the growers of rice, enticed planters to start groves of quinine trees, and invited immigrants to bring their know-how and capital to his country, hoping that they would become good Guatemalans.

Without an adequate labor force Barrios' ambitious development schemes would have died on the vine. To assure the necessary *brazos*, vagrancy laws made all eligible males enter the work force. And because three fourths of Guatemala's population was Indian, the labor program of necessity involved the delineation of an Indian policy. Like earlier liberals, Barrios' goal was to integrate the Indian—to encourage him to put on the shoes and dress of the *ladino* and get him off his communal lands, to give him an individual title and hope that he would become more than a subsistence producer of food.

More important, and typical of the *patrón's* view that Indians were lazy and improvident, Barrios outlined a forced labor program similar to the *mandamientos* of the colonial period.[5] Despite provisions to protect the Indians from abuse, the laws ruthlessly supported the landowners and permitted a vicious debt peonage to develop. Regardless of their status as *jornaleros* (wage labor) or *mozos colonos* (tenant farmers), the Indians lived in virtual slavery, abused by their *patrones* and by *habilitadores* (labor contractors), who herded them everywhere. There was nothing liberal or humane about the Indian program Barrios formulated; the 1894 Law of Workers, passed by Barrios successors, further tightened the noose around the necks of the hapless Indian.[6] Landowners and foreign corporations welcomed the government's measures.

By modern standards it might seem that Barrios made excessive concessions to entrepreneurs, both foreign and domestic. But it is only fair to judge him by nineteenth-century standards. Untapped national resources were of no value to anyone, he reasoned. And if the state regulated the process of exploitation, abuses would be reduced to a minimum. As the economy prospered, the interested par-

[5] Burgess, *op. cit.*, p. 163, reproduces Barrios' circular of November 3, 1876, to the political chiefs.

[6] Dana G. Munro, *The Five Republics of Central America: Their Political and Economic Development and Their Relations with the United States* (New York, 1918), pp. 59-69.

ties callously overlooked the social and human abuses of the new order: it was the price one had to pay for material progress. What he did for Guatemala Barrios tried to do for all of Central America. In his travels to Europe and the United States he had been impressed by the unity movements of Bismark and Cavour and by the results of union in the Northern republic, its way of life and its stable economy. With her tremendous economic potential Central America too could become a leading power of the world, and Justo Rufino Barrios would be remembered by history as the patriot who launched the *patria grande* on her career to greatness. On February 28, 1885, the son of Los Altos electrified Central America with his pronouncement for union: the time was at hand for Central Americans to close ranks in a unitary republic, eliminating once and for all the humiliating weakness of disunity. Those who did not accept this call were traitors and should be treated as such.

As might be expected, Barrios' sudden and dramatic plea for union shook the foundations of Central America. Guatemalans hailed their leader's announcement; Luis Bográn of Honduras promptly fell into line; unionists everywhere pressured their governments to follow suit. But many politicians shuddered at the prospect of becoming mere satellites of the Guatemalan strongman. Traditionally isolationist, Costa Rica marshaled her forces for the showdown. So did Nicaragua's conservative regime, alarmed at the possibility of having liberalism forced upon it by a strong central government. Porfirio Díaz of Mexico deployed troops along the Guatemalan border and encouraged defiance of Barrios' call; a powerful neighbor to the south was not to his liking. The opposition to union gained precious time because of the stalling tactics of Rafael Zaldívar, the Salvadorean president who owed his office to Barrios. When the glove fell, Barrios led his troops to the Salvadorean border. On April 2, 1885, a sharpshooter's bullet struck him down. He died instantly, three months shy of his fiftieth birthday. Another attempt at union had failed.[7]

Barrios' program of "peace, education, and material prosperity"

[7] Burgess, *op. cit.*, pp. 238-86; and John D. Martz, *Justo Rufino Barrios and Central American Union* (Gainesville, 1963), pp. 8-51, which is the most recent evaluation of Barrios' unionist efforts.

established the pattern for modern Central America, though not all his contemporaries and successors practiced it with the same fervor and intentions. Nationalistic objectives almost everywhere gave way to selfish considerations. This was the case in Barrios' own country under the so-called liberal governments of Manuel Lisandro Barillas (1885-92), José Maria Barrios, the "Reformer's" nephew, (1892-98), and Manuel Estrada Cabrera (1898-1920), a vicious tyrant. By fraud and chicanery they twisted the constitution of 1879 to perpetuate their power, especially Estrada Cabrera, and to benefit personally from the economic forces their predecessor had set in motion. In short, Guatemalan liberalism went bankrupt in the six decades following Barrios' death. The same phenomenon occurred elsewhere in Central America.

The reforms of Justo Rufino Barrios and others, coupled with the industrial transformation of Western Europe and the United States which created an almost insatiable demand for raw materials during the second half of the nineteenth century, helped to fix the stamp of monoculture on Central America's economy. New products replaced cochineal and indigo, which by the end of the 1850s could no longer compete with Europe's chemical dyes. The major exchange-getters now were coffee and bananas, and because they required large outlays of money, the big plantation owned by foreign corporations and enterprising families of Central America became characteristic. The heavy emphasis on large-scale commercial agriculture thus perpetuated the social patterns of the past in a more demanding and impersonal form. The invaluable allies of the landed oligarchy, the foreign capitalists, whose numbers increased noticeably, insisted upon stable and friendly governments that made prosperity possible.

Coffee culture found a natural environment in Central America. Costa Rica was the first to grow the tasty bean in the 1830s, expanding her production in the second half of the century as communications were opened up to Puntarenas on the Pacific and Puerto Limón on the Atlantic. El Salvador began her career as the leading coffee producer of Central America under Gerardo Barrios (1860-63), capitalizing on the advantages of terrain that facilitated transportation. Thanks to Justo Rufino Barrios, Guatemala joined the race for coffee profits in the 1870s; so did Nicaragua. Only Honduras lacked the proper conditions to grow coffee. Central Americans maintained a competitive position in the world market by paying low wages to labor, thus offsetting the higher transportation costs that a rugged terrain imposed upon them.

By the end of the nineteenth century the rising demand for bananas in the United States, along with improvements in storage facilities and navigation, gave the Central American countries a special advantage in growing that product. The hitherto depopulated and unproductive lowlands of the Caribbean coast now came into their own. Honduras led in banana production until 1935 when the *sigatoka* disease ravaged her plantations. Guatemala, Nicaragua, and Costa Rica likewise received substantial revenues from the banana industry, an enterprise dominated by foreign companies from the start. Although at first many firms vied for the banana traffic, the trend toward consolidation began early. The Vaccaro brothers of New Orleans formed the Standard Fruit and Steamship Company in 1924; five years later the United Fruit Company (UFCO), founded in 1899, bought out the Cuyamel Fruit Company of the enterprising Samuel Zemurray from Mobile, Alabama. With influence in many quarters and considerable financial backing, these two banana empires wielded immense power in the countries where they operated, oftentimes to the detriment of the local citizenry, giving rise to the stereotype of the "Banana Republics" of Central America.

Foreign control and influence was an inevitable concomitant of Central America's decision to modernize by joining the mainstream of world trade. Since domestic capitalists lacked the money, experience, and will to construct railroads, bridges, utilities, and communications, foreigners stepped into the gap. They built and owned the capital goods of the nation, operated the most efficient plantations that produced the bulk of the exports, and, for better or for worse, controlled the banking institutions of the country. Even the retail trade came under their dominion. So it is not surprising that they exerted their powerful influence on governments to maintain domestic stability, assure them of cheap labor, and grant them concessions that compensated them for the risks involved.

In the hurly-burly of profit gathering, ethical standards often went by the board—a moral breakdown that was not one-sided, however. Realizing the moment of a lifetime to amass a personal fortune, unscrupulous *politicos* gave exorbitant concessions and privileges to foreigners who openly solicited them. Considering the many opportunities of the day, government thus became a lucrative business for aspiring politicians who dreamed up ingenious ways of continuing their control of office—the process of *continuismo* that students of Latin American government cite often. The essence and motive of the *personalista* age in Central American history was to follow a political boss who could deliver, and would distribute, the spoils of office. The rare exceptions to the rule were voices in the wilderness, unheard and unheeded.

While world trade ran smoothly, the interested parties applauded economic progress, complimented themselves on being "the fittest" in the struggle for survival, and blamed the abuses of the system on the "Iron Laws" of wages and supply-and-demand. But in the final decade of the nineteenth century the panic in the financial markets of the world, leading to a tightening of credit sources and a drop in commodity prices, exposed the weaknesses of economies which depended too heavily on foreign financing and on the fate of one or two products in world trade.

Central America's financial structure was severely jarred by world developments from 1890 to 1920—the beginning of serious problems that area has had to face ever since. During the course of the nineteenth century her foreign and domestic debts multiplied at an alarming rate, and Costa Rica and El Salvador were the only states which managed to settle their accounts with British bondholders for their shares of the Republic's debts. Refunding schemes and loans for railroad construction and other enterprises of the 1870s and 1880s had increased the total indebtedness to foreigners. While coffee prices followed an upward trend, Central American governments, with the notable exception of Honduras, met the service charges on their debts. Because of the financial crisis of the 1890s, however, many of them were forced to default, especially in 1894. Refunding loans usually followed such interruptions in payments, and creditors had no choice but to scale down their claims if they wanted any returns at all. In the process, the credit ratings of Central American countries suffered; bondholders lost their patience and threatened force.

It was not just "a listless sense of national honor" that prevented Central Americans from meeting their financial obligations, a point that Professor Dana G. Munro has underscored.[8] Oftentimes there was reasonable doubt to question the validity of loans that had been negotiated under suspicious circumstances. Such were the Costa Rican loans of 1871 and 1872. Honduras also considered seriously the repudiation of bonds (1867-70) for the construction of the National Railway from Puerto Cortés to the Gulf of Fonseca, the proceeds of which, once government officials and the speculators floating the loan had subtracted their "commissions," permitted the laying of 90 kilometers of road! And because the Honduran government demurred, its credit rating fell to zero, retarding the country's economic progress until the banana boom of the twentieth century.

Inflation likewise added to the predicament faced by Central Americans, and not all of it was of their own making. Financial systems pegged to silver suffered from the drop in the world's price of that commodity, and total indebtedness spiraled in terms of local currencies. The decline in coffee prices, furthermore, brought with it a sharp drop in government revenues. A weakening of the major source of income led governments to the practice of issuing irredeemable paper money, and the value of the local currencies depreciated even more. The dislocation of international trade that accompanied World War I also complicated matters for Central Americans, many of whom now began to realize the vulnerability of overspecialization in agriculture.

The Age of Zelaya (1893-1909)

Liberalism remained a powerful force in Central America after the death of Justo Rufino Barrios, especially the watered-down variety. In El Salvador, Rafael Zaldívar resigned his position shortly after the victory, and Francisco Menéndez, the leader of the Salvadorean unionists in 1885, replaced him. Luis Bográn, Guatemala's only ally in that debacle, held power in Honduras until 1891, and

[8] Munro, *The Five Republics*, p. 295; also see his excellent analysis of Central American debts, pp. 262-95.

Bernardo Soto (1886-90) introduced key educational and political reforms into Costa Rica. In Nicaragua the conservative regime reached a turning point in 1889 when President Evaristo Carazo died in office and was succeeded by his Leonese vice-president Roberto Sacasa. Two years later Sacasa was elected to a term in his own right. The conservative coalition which had maintained the peace in Nicaragua for over three decades fell apart when Sacasa proceeded to select Leonese friends for major posts in his administration, thus reviving the historic feud between León and Granada. Capitalizing upon the disunity of their adversaries, the liberals resumed control of the government in 1893 under the capable leadership of José Santos Zelaya, a young politician from Managua. For the next 16 years he was the dominant figure of Nicaragua and of all Central America, replacing Barrios as the president-maker of the area.

As many historians have noted, Zelaya and Barrios had a great deal in common. Both were positivists in their emphasis upon public secular education and had to contend with the powerful influence of the Church in their respective countries. Both worshipped economic progress. Both were modern-day nationalists who had a vision of the greater *patria* (fatherland) in which they hoped to play the lead, and both men were autocrats at heart, having little interest in effective democratic government. Zelaya, however, much like Barrios' successors in Guatemala, regarded political office as the occasion for personal enrichment, and his economic projects represented a continuation and expansion of the trend his conservative predecessors had started in the 1880s—the railroad building that tied the western half of the nation together and the subsidizing of coffee culture. Above all, Zelaya was a master politician in playing off factions and localities against each other. Like Barrios and his native highlands, Zelaya deliberately built up the importance of Managua in Nicaraguan life, and it became more than a compromise capital between the warring municipalities of León and Granada.

Like his Guatemalan counterpart, Zelaya consolidated his political position and protected his country by intervening in the affairs of his neighbors, surrounding himself with men who agreed with him. In 1893, for example, he helped the liberal Policarpo Bonilla gain control of the Honduran government after a two-year lapse of conservative rule that followed the elections of 1891, and in 1894 he had perhaps more than a passing interest in the Salvadorean coup of Rafael Gutiérrez. With the center securely in the liberal column and a sympathetic government in Guatemala, it would seem that Central America was ripe for another attempt at union. Only in Costa Rica, where Bernardo Soto permitted free elections in 1889—a landmark in Costa Rican political history—were the conservatives in charge, first under José Joaquín Rodríguez (1890-94) and then under Rafael Iglesias (1894-1902).

Zelaya's national and regional prestige was further enhanced by the incorporation of the Mosquito reservation in 1894, leading to a diplomatic showdown with the British, who, according to the 1860 treaty, were responsible for guaranteeing the existence of that reserve—England's last link to her former protectorate on the Mosquito Shore. When the British consul complained, Zelaya expelled him from Nicaragua, to the plaudits of countrymen throughout Central America. Insisting upon an indemnity for this insult to the British flag, the English blockaded the port of Corinto in 1895. At this point the United States government intervened and brought about a settlement: Nicaragua paid the indemnity and England recognized the unqualified sovereignty of the Nicaraguan government over the reservation area. Hailed as a national hero, Zelaya had no trouble asserting his will over the politicians from León, who had hoped to dominate the young Managuan, in the elections of 1896. He was now undisputed ruler of Nicaragua.

Great Britain's blockade of Corinto aided the unionist cause. This foreign threat led to the formation of another central government called the *República Mayor*, or Greater Republic of Central America, a loose confederation that represented the three center states in diplomatic relations and lasted from 1895 to 1898. Like its predecessors of 1844 and 1851, which were also responses to foreign threats, the Greater Republic led a tremulous existence. The signatory states were not really interested in giving the general government any effective authority and support, and Costa Rica and Guatemala, for reasons of their own, refused to join the pact despite the blandishments offered to President Iglesias of Costa Rica. Finally a Salvadorean *caudillo*, Tomás Regalado, overthrew the Gutiérrez government and took El Salvador out of the "United States of Central America," the name adopted under the new constitution that went into effect on November 1, 1898.[9] In short, all the ingredients of previous failures were in the concoction of the 1890s in perhaps a more exaggerated form because of the growth of state nationalism over the passing years.

Yet there was a salutary reaction to this latest failure of unionism because more and more Central Americans, and especially the youth, came to realize that unionism under existing conditions was impossible. Beginning in 1899 Guatemalan students, led by such stalwarts as Salvador Mendieta, began a crusade to enlighten Central America on the benefits of union—an educational program to develop a regional consciousness. In many respects this youth movement, which gained adherents in all five countries of Central America and formed the *Partido Unionista* in 1904, represented a revival of the old *Morazanista* program.[10] Determined to form a genuine Central American nation—it was futile to work through the existing governmental structures—these young men hoped to achieve their cherished objective by appealing to the intellect and heart of their countrymen. Their approach would be apolitical, and the means peaceful. Moreover, Central America's youth was reacting to the materialistic emphasis of the "new liberalism" and the accompanying disregard for effective democratic institutions. The impact of the crusade upon Central America was undoubtedly profound; it gave new meaning to unionism and perhaps may have influenced the trend toward a peaceful settlement of differences among the states of Central America. Certainly, it conditioned the minds of future Central American statesmen and political leaders, and the effects can be seen in the present unionist movement.

In 1902 President Zelaya again tried to rally the states to unionism by inviting their leaders to a meeting at Corinto. Four presidents answered the call, and in the treaty that followed they accepted the principle of arbitration by establishing a special regional tribunal to

[9] Thomas L. Karnes, *The Failure of Union: Central America, 1824-1960* (Chapel Hill, 1961), pp. 167-74.
[10] *Ibid.*, pp. 204-6, for an excellent analysis of this movement.

settle all their disputes. Although the immediate results were not gratifying, the precedent was an important one for the next two decades. A bad omen at the time was Guatemala's refusal to join the peace machinery set up at Corinto. Much of Central America's subsequent instability derived from the suspicions and rivalry of Manuel Estrada Cabrera and José Santos Zelaya. Since Porfirio Díaz of Mexico likewise feared a strong Guatemala, he proved to be Zelaya's natural ally, a development that complicated the peace efforts from 1906 forward.

While Central American executives were outlining their peace machinery at Corinto, the United States arrived at the conclusion that it could no longer be a passive spectator of events in Central America, a decision timed to coincide with its commitment to build a waterway across the Isthmus. During the second half of the nineteenth century, while the Northern republic matured to an industrial giant and created a powerful naval arm, the Clayton-Bulwer Treaty had blocked the Isthmian ambitions of the young country. England simply would not yield the legal point, as James G. Blaine learned in the early 1880s. The contract was binding; the United States could not dominate or fortify a canal of its own in the area. American frustration reached the breaking point when a French company undertook the construction of the vaunted passageway, though that project soon languished.

In the meantime, naval authorities of Alfred Mahan's stature were emphasizing the strategic importance of the Caribbean and the imperative need to control an Isthmian passageway if their country was to take its place among the leading powers of the world. Other voices exaggerated the German threat to the Monroe Doctrine at the turn of the century and raised the specter of European intervention in the New World to collect the debts that unruly Latin American governments owed to creditors overseas. The United States could not, and should not, they said, tolerate such action even if it meant an American guarantee of the stability of Middle American countries. Finally, in the Hay-Pauncefote Treaty of November 18, 1901, Great Britain released the United States from the inhibition of the 1850 treaty. The big question now was the location of the prospective canal.

Despite the skillful lobbying of agents representing French interests in Panama, it was generally assumed, at least before 1902, that the canal would be built through Nicaragua, following the San Juan River to the western lakes. Although this was a longer and more expensive route, the United States did not have to contend with any existing company, as they would have to in Panama. The Nicaraguan route, however, did involve negotiations with two Central American countries because Costa Rica had riparian rights to the San Juan River by virtue of the 1858 treaty with Nicaragua and the 1888 arbitral award of President Grover Cleveland. And the Costa Rican negotiations occasioned delays, for the *Ticos* argued that an amendment to their constitution was a prerequisite for any contract. In May 1903 the Costa Rican congress rejected such an amendment.

President Zelaya's nationalism and sensitivity, however well founded, likewise obstructed the negotiations. He adamantly refused to accept the demand for extraterritorial rights such as the establishment of American courts in the canal zone to try cases involving citizens of the United States. After some bargaining Zelaya agreed to a cash payment of $6 million, and a contract was drawn up in December 1901. But the State Department found it unacceptable because it did not include a provision for judicial autonomy in the canal area.[11] An impasse followed in which the advocates of the Panama route gained the advantage. The United States then shifted its attention to Bogotá, Colombia. Of course, Zelaya reacted angrily to the change of events; yet, considering Nicaraguans' recollections of the Chatfield era, it is not difficult to understand why they would not yield on the issue of extraterritorial rights. It proved to be an expensive and fateful defense of principle.

The controversial events that led to Panamanian independence from Colombia on November 3, 1903, are too well known to merit repetition here. The United States recognized the new country two days later and on the 18th negotiated the treaty that permitted the construction of the Panama Canal. In early 1904 an article in the Panamanian constitution gave the United States the right of intervention in the internal affairs of the young nation. These basic facts

[11] Dana G. Munro, *Intervention and Dollar Diplomacy in the Caribbean, 1900-1921* (Princeton, 1964), pp. 40-41.

and the subsequent remarks of President Theodore Roosevelt, not to mention the maneuvers of the American navy, tended to confirm the widespread belief throughout Latin America that United States' "imperialism" was on the march. Certainly the disgruntled Zelaya preferred to think that this was true and acted accordingly. In possession of the Panama Canal Zone, the United States was now doubly interested in preserving the peace in Central America, for the security of the canal itself was at stake.

The year 1903 was a crucial one for Central America. Not only did it mark the beginning of the United States' active participation in the area but also the start of two troublesome currents that kept Central Americans distracted for the next five years. First, there was the threat of war between Estrada Cabrera of Guatemala and Tomás Regalado of El Salvador, the typical struggle of *caudillos* who were fighting because of personal whim rather than any state objectives. Zelaya, on the other hand, was playing one enemy off against the other—Regalado, who had frustrated the *República Mayor*, and Estrada Cabrera, who was the major challenger to Zelaya's ambitions in Central America. President Roosevelt, hoping to avert war, offered to mediate; the proposal was rejected. Other attempts to prevent the outbreak of war under the terms of the Corinto Treaty of 1902 merely delayed hostilities until mid-1906, when Guatemalan *emigrados* from four Central American states converged on Guatemala to oust Estrada Cabrera. Regalado lost his life in the invasion; his death in turn weakened the Salvadorean government, creating a power vacuum that inevitably would tempt Zelaya.

A second powder keg was lit in Honduras in 1903 when Manuel Bonilla took over the government by force, ending the rule of liberals like Policarpo Bonilla (1893-99) and his hand-picked successor Terencio Sierra (1899-1903), whom Zelaya had aided to power. A conservative, this new Bonilla (who was not related to the former President) constituted another threat to Zelaya's position in Nicaragua and his hopes of uniting the five states of Central America. The intrigue to undermine Bonilla's rule bore fruit in December 1906, when rebels pronounced against the government, undoubtedly with the support of *Zelayistas*. In chasing the revolutionaries Honduran troops violated Nicaraguan soil. Zelaya demanded reparations, and when these were not forthcoming, he invaded Honduras in force. On March 18, 1907, at the Battle of Namasigue (incidentally, machine guns made their first appearance in Central America at this time) Nicaraguan troops toppled the Bonilla government, and Zelaya selected Miguel Dávila to head the new regime.

At this point, the two currents that had been initiated four years earlier came together. Estrada Cabrera readied his troops to stop the spread of Zelaya's influence. The Salvadorean government under Fernando Figueroa, who only a year before had fought Guatemala, now reluctantly joined Estrada Cabrera to combat *Zelayista* subversion and an invasion attempt by Nicaraguan troops. In the various peace conferences that followed, Zelaya maintained that his major objective was Central American union, yet his moves created the opposite result.

In conjunction with Porfirio Díaz of Mexico and the neutral states of Central America, Theodore Roosevelt urged the 1906 belligerents to discuss their differences aboard the U.S.S. *Marblehead* off the Salvadorean coast. Hostilities ceased for the time being, and the states agreed to meet again in San José, Costa Rica, in September. Only Zelaya refused to participate in the San José meetings, on the ground that the United States had no right to intervene in Central American affairs. Nevertheless, the conference was constructive in reaffirming the Corinto Treaty of 1902, which had set up a peace tribunal. The delegates favored the establishment of two institutions that would help foment unionism in Central America: the Pedagogical Institute in San José and the International Central American Bureau in Guatemala City. The Bureau opened for business on September 15, 1907, and, influenced by the *Partido Unionista*, it became a powerful weapon for spreading the gospel of unionism throughout Central America, so much so that jealous state governments reduced it to impotence in 1910.[12]

The peace efforts of 1906, however, were only important for the precedents set; they certainly did not stop the warfare of 1907, described above. At Zelaya's request—it would seem that the failure of his Salvadorean invasion had a sobering effect upon him—Porfirio Díaz proposed another peace gathering. The United States concurred,

[12] Karnes, *op. cit.*, pp. 196-97.

and the delegates met in Washington from November 14 to December 20, 1907. The treaties and conventions signed at Washington set the guideposts for the conduct of Central American affairs during the next decade. By encouraging the meeting, Mexico and the United States added their moral support to the results of the conference, thereby assuming a certain responsibility for the implementation of its terms.

Central Americans faced the problem of establishing peace with some realism, judging from the conventions signed in Washington; whether or not they would be willing to implement the program outlined was another matter. Reaffirming earlier agreements, they decided to set up in Cartago, Costa Rica, a Central American Court of Justice for a ten-year period, empowered to judge and enforce its decisions in all cases brought before it affecting the peace of the area. Delegates also agreed on the neutralization of Honduras, a tempting power vacuum in Central America's historical record since independence; the curtailment of hostile action by *emigrados*; the extradition of criminals; the nonrecognition of regimes that obtained power by illegal means; nonintervention in each other's affairs; and intimate cultural and economic ties by supporting the International Central American Bureau and the Pedagogical Institute established earlier at San José.

Away from the peace table, however, Central Americans reverted to the habits of decades. Estrada Cabrera had little confidence in Zelaya's proclamations of altruism, and the Nicaraguan President had grounds to doubt the sincerity of his Guatemalan enemy. In mid-1908 revolutionists moved into Honduras from bases in Guatemala and El Salvador, determined to oust the Dávila government. Zelaya, of course, came to his ally's rescue, and a general war seemed imminent as Honduras and Nicaragua charged El Salvador and Guatemala of duplicity by encouraging the rebels. Fortunately, Costa Rica invoked the Washington treaties and urged the contenders to submit their cases to the Court of Justice in Cartago. They agreed, and war was thus averted, a significant triumph for the peace movement of Central America. The judges' votes, however, followed national lines— two for and two against. Costa Rica broke the deadlock by voting to absolve Guatemala and El Salvador of responsibility for the invasion. The Court had stopped a war, but the decision weakened its prestige, for it was commonly assumed, and with considerable justification, that Estrada Cabrera had violated the Washington treaties.

As secretary of state under President Theodore Roosevelt from July 1905 to January 1909, Elihu Root helped shape and implement the administration's policy toward Latin countries in the strategic Middle American area, coloring it with a sympathetic understanding of Latin American personality and sensitivity. To protect the Panama Canal, which was Roosevelt's primary objective, it was necessary to maintain stability in the area and prevent intervention by outside powers. Hence the Roosevelt Corollary of the Monroe Doctrine, announced in December 1904, which arrogated to the United States the right to intervene in those countries where order was breaking down or a threat of outside interference was likely—a policy of "preventive imperialism," as some authorities have called it. Working out peace programs such as those described above for Central America, establishing customs receiverships (as was done in the Dominican Republic), and making arrangements to secure the fiscal solvency of a nation—in all these ways Root tried to accomplish the major objective. Hoping to avoid the impression of overbearing American influence, he deliberately sought Mexico's cooperation in maintaining the peace of Central America despite, or because of, that nation's sympathy for the Zelaya regime and Porfirio Díaz' determination to undermine the influence of his Northern neighbor in the area. In short, Root's means were commendable and reflect upon his sincerity of purpose: to maintain the peace for strategic reasons as well as for the encouragement of American trade and investment.[13]

But Root was not able to solve the problem posed by José Santos Zelaya, the hostile President of Nicaragua whose grievances toward the United States dated back to the abrupt ending of canal negotiations. Personal resentment, and perhaps anger at himself for having insisted too strenuously on the nationalistic principle of Nicaraguan courts, seem to have been the motives for his arbitrary actions against the American community in Nicaragua. He canceled the Weil concession to collect import duties on liquor and the Emery woodcutting contract and threatened American mining interests with

[13] Munro, *Intervention*, pp. 112-16.

similar action. The heated controversy and the insulting language he used with the United States' minister led to a serious diplomatic break by late 1908, when a minor agent was left in charge of the legation. In that year, moreover, there were rumors that Zelaya was urging a Japanese company to construct a rival canal through Nicaragua and that he had also opened negotiations with the British to cede the Great Corn Island to them.

That was the situation when Philander C. Knox assumed command of the State Department in early 1909 under the administration of President William Howard Taft. Unlike Root, this seasoned lawyer was not familiar with Latin America, nor did he seem to be friendly or sympathetic to the ways of the Spanish world.[14] Understandably, he was especially affected by the emotional block that had developed in Washington circles about José Santos Zelaya, that unruly Yankee-phobe who was causing all the trouble in Central America, insulting United States ministers, canceling *bona fide* contracts—sin of all sins to a legal mind—and threatening to encourage a competitor to the American canal in Panama. Then, in May 1909, Zelaya negotiated a loan with English and French bankers (the Ethelburga Syndicate of London) for £1,250,000 to provide funds for a railroad to the Atlantic coast. Since 1895, incidentally, Zelaya had scrupulously paid the interest on the foreign debt; the bankers therefore welcomed the transaction despite Knox's vain efforts to thwart it.

When a revolution broke out in October 1909 against the Zelaya government, Knox minced no words about his sympathy for the rebels. Whether intentional or not, the actions of American officials and naval officers added substance to the common belief that the United States government had sponsored the uprising and was doing its best to keep it alive—charges that a recent study has refuted in a convincing manner.[15] Recognizing the ill will of the United States, Zelaya resigned from the presidency of his country on December 16, 1909, ending his controversial 16-year stint in Central America's spotlight. A political untouchable, Zelaya faded into obscurity. To many Central Americans he is one of the area's great heroes—an emotional fact worth pondering.

[14] *Ibid.*, pp. 160-61.
[15] *Ibid.*, pp. 167-86.

The Big Stick (1909-1933)

Under Philander C. Knox the spirit of United States' policy in Central America took a different turn from which it did not substantially deviate until the 1930s. Unlike his predecessor, Knox chose to ignore Mexico and embarked upon a unilateral program of keeping the peace in the strategic Middle American zone. The parallels with the Chatfield era were striking. A powerful English-speaking nation, which, like Britain, took for granted its racial and cultural superiority, imposed its will upon Central America using similar means: the deployment of naval forces almost constantly on both coasts; the landing of marines, on occasion, to protect the lives and property of nationals as well as to buttress constituted governments; the insistence upon customs collectorships and financial reforms; and the preference for conservative regimes, which represented the respectable and law-abiding elements in Central America. There were, of course, twentieth-century elaborations such as the refunding schemes by which American bankers replaced their European counterparts, thus averting outside intervention in Central America—this was the "dollar diplomacy" of the Taft administration—and the training of local constabularies by American personnel, a contribution of the Wilson administration.

To this day there is considerable controversy about the motives underlying American policy of that period. A careful perusal of documents in State Department archives reveals the political objective: the defense of the Panama Canal by maintaining stability through the means described above. The establishment of order, in turn, would promote economic, cultural, and political progress. Some scholars, however, question the good intentions of the United States and regard them as a rationalization for baser economic motives— monopolies for American bankers, exclusive contracts, and so forth. Drawing heavily from liberal sources, these critics infer a great deal, perhaps too much, from the consequences of the policy. As usual, the illusive truth lies somewhere in the middle.

Despite the argument concerning motives, the general consensus is that American policy actually did more harm than good during the years in question even though it brought some relief from the dis-

orders of the earlier period, especially from 1912 to 1917. Fiscal reforms, however, did not meet expectations, and by 1913, most State
Department experts were disillusioned with customs collectorships
as a panecea for underdeveloped countries. Close supervision of the
political processes, moreover, undermined the ability of Central
American leaders to assume responsibility—hardly the best preparation for eventual self-government. The poor caliber of diplomatic
representatives in the field further weakened the United States'
policy.[16]

More importantly, the undemocratic means and the attitude of
superiority that accompanied the implementation of the American
program was offensive to the national pride of Central Americans and
fostered a fund of hatred, or Yankeephobia, that has endured to the
present day. Ultranationalists and enemies of the United States have
exploited this fault in the psychological structure of the Latin American mind to their own advantage. Liberals in particular, who had
been our allies in the nineteenth-century conflict with Chatfield and
his crowd, felt betrayed by the United States. No wonder they attributed the historic reversal to ulterior motives.

From the start of the anti-Zelaya revolution Central Americans
keenly resented the imperious attitude of American officials toward
the President of Nicaragua. Regardless of the adjectives and argu-
ments State Department spokesmen used to justify their views—
Zelaya the unscrupulous tyrant, demon, and cause of "constant tension and turmoil" in Central America—their oversimplified analysis
of regional strife failed to convince those persons who knew better.
After all, Estrada Cabrera, not Zelaya, had broken the peace pacts
of 1907. Nicaragua's financial record was not the weakest in Central
America; why then the urgency for a customs collectorship and
fiscal reforms? To these minds it appeared that anti-Zelayismo was
merely the angry reaction of a powerful English-speaking nation
toward a Latin President who dared to question the right of North
Americans to interfere in regional matters and to assert the equality
and sovereignty of his nation. Difficult to prove, this suspicion that
the United States was bullying a weaker neighbor fanned the embers
of Yankeephobia throughout Central America. This is an aspect of

[16] *Ibid.*, pp. 530-46, presents a masterly review of the policy.

American policy in Nicaragua that has not been treated with the thoroughness it deserves. Further research along these lines may expose a hitherto unsuspected dimension to the controversy over motivation.

Secretary of State Knox certainly performed like a man obsessed with Zelaya and everyone connected with him. A good example of this was his note of December 1, 1909, which in turn influenced President Taft's annual message to Congress a week later, containing sentiments that ordinarily do not characterize diplomatic correspondence.[17] Hoping to placate the injured feelings of the Northern power, and doubtlessly at the suggestion of Porfirio Díaz, Zelaya resigned from the presidency and left a fellow liberal, José Madriz, in command. But the United States rejected this compromise move, refused to recognize the Madriz government, and chose to ignore Mexico as a partner in keeping the peace of Central America. As a result, Madriz could not sustain himself beyond August 28, 1910, especially since American vessels had restricted his ability to cope with the rebels. Recognition was accorded, however, to the rebel government of Juan J. Estrada, the liberal ex-governor of Oriente who had declared against Zelaya at Bluefields.[18]

In the power struggle that followed the main contenders were the conservative generals Luis Mena and Emiliano Chamorro; Estrada and his vice-president Adolf Díaz likewise sought to ingratiate themselves with the all-powerful State Department. Estrada fell in late 1911; Díaz took over and, hopeful of securing his position, asked the United States government in December for a "Platt Amendment," which would have made Nicaragua in effect a protectorate of the United States. Estrada and Díaz agreed submissively to a funding scheme, a customs collectorship, and a mixed commission of two North Americans and one Nicaraguan to adjudicate outstanding claims. As a moderate conservative who had been identified with American mining interests, Adolf Díaz was acceptable to the United States. When Mena rebelled against him in July 1912, Díaz and Chamorro joined forces. Then Mena made the mistake of accepting

[17] *Ibid.*, pp. 176-77. It was President Taft who used the phrase "constant tension and turmoil" in referring to Zelaya.
[18] *Ibid.*, pp. 177-79, 183-84, 189.

the support of dissident liberals from León, thereby raising the bugaboo of *Zelayismo*. At Díaz' request, and to fight a "regime of barbarity and corruption," [19] United States Marines entered the fray in late August 1912. In less than two months the war was over. One hundred marines stayed on as a legation guard for the next 13 years, a symbol of the United States' determination to keep the peace in Central America. Uncluttered with the presence of liberals, the election of late 1912 went to the faithful Díaz, who began a four-year term on New Year's Day.

The real power among the conservatives, Emiliano Chamorro went off to Washington where he made many friends. Not to be denied, however, he ran for the presidency of his country in 1916. Still obsessed with *Zelayismo*, the State Department refused to sanction the candidacy of Julián Irías, the leading liberal contender who had come to Washington to assure American officials that he would be cooperative. Instead, Chamorro was escorted back to Nicaragua on a U.S. warship.[20] Díaz challenged his bid for power, but Chamorro won the elections, by the use of fraud. Unable to run again in 1920 because of the constitutional inhibition, Chamorro pushed the cause of his uncle, Diego Manuel Chamorro. Fraud again decided the outcome, despite American efforts to prevent it. Guilty consciences or embarrassed officials in the State Department exacted a promise from the strong-willed Chamorro that the elections in 1924 would be honest and at the same time announced that the legation guard would be withdrawn shortly after that election.

In the meantime, "dollar diplomacy" had failed to uplift other governments of Central America. Thanks to connections with banana company executives, Manuel Bonilla, Zelaya's old enemy, regained power in Honduras. When Bonilla died in 1913, Francisco Bertrand held sway until 1919; armed resistance ended his attempt to put a relative in office. Nationalistic pressures, moreover, prevented any fiscal reforms or funding schemes from gaining congressional approval.

Despite the presence of American warships, which brought temporary relief on occasions, the state governments continued to meddle in each other's affairs. Estrada Cabrera of Guatemala was a special

[19] *Ibid.*, p. 207.
[20] *Ibid.*, pp. 406-10.

nuisance to the State Department, a despot who made many promises but never kept them. And in 1917 a revolutionary government under Federico Tinoco captured control in Costa Rica. For two years he defied the nonrecognition policy of President Woodrow Wilson, who insisted on this tact to discourage illegal seizures of power. Finally, Tinoco was forced from office, but by then, and considering the successful coup in Honduras, it was clear that the United States was no longer keeping the peace in Central America.

In the eyes of Central Americans, the United States' insistence upon the negotiation of a canal-option treaty with a submissive Nicaraguan government was especially humiliating and offensive, an uncalled-for display of the might-makes-right thesis in foreign relations. The impact of those negotiations was indeed unfortunate, arousing suspicions about American designs without furthering the genuine interests of the United States in the area. Even today, the memory of that ill-advised action lingers on in the minds of millions in Latin America who have read *The Shark and the Sardines* by Juan José Arévalo, the ex-president of Guatemala. It is not surprising that Fidel Castro has chosen to propagate the notion that the "sardines" have nothing in common with their voracious neighbor.[21]

Following the first intervention of American marines in Nicaragua, the American minister, George T. Weitzel, met secretly with General Chamorro; they signed the Chamorro-Weitzel Convention on February 8, 1913. By its terms the United States gained the right, in perpetuity, to construct a canal through Nicaragua, and, to protect the approaches to the Panama Canal, it also received 99-year leases, renewable for an equivalent term, to the Great Corn Island and the Little Corn Island in the Caribbean, as well as the right to construct a naval base on the Gulf of Fonseca for the same number of years. In return, Nicaragua would receive a payment of $3 million. When the news leaked out, Central Americans charged angrily that it was a deliberate attempt to wreck the union movement and an act of treachery that lowered the gates to an "American invasion." [22] They sent their protests to congressmen in Washington, to the State De-

[21] *The Shark and the Sardines*, by Juan José Arévalo (New York, 1961), was written shortly after the fall of Arbenz and has run through several printings Castro has supported the English translation.

[22] New York *Times*, July 23 and December 15, 1913.

partment, and to the American press. The distractions of an election year postponed congressional action on the convention.

When the Wilson administration took over, it continued the policies of its predecessor despite its alleged antipathy to "dollar diplomacy." Indeed, Secretary of State William Jennings Bryan seemed to have forgotten his former anti-imperialist views and chose to add the equivalent of the "Platt Amendment" to the Chamorro-Weitzel pact, envisioning a virtual protectorate of Nicaragua. In the face of resistance he dropped the Weitzel document altogether, and on August 5, 1914, he negotiated a new convention, the Bryan-Chamorro Treaty—identical to the previous one, as it first appeared —which the Senate ratified on February 18, 1916.

Central Americans were infuriated by these moves on the part of a Democratic administration, which they had hoped would erase the errors of the past. Even Colombians protested that Nicaragua had no right to alienate the Corn islands, which belonged to them by virtue of an 1803 Spanish decree. Costa Rica reminded the State Department that Nicaragua had violated the Cañas-Jérez Treaty of 1858, the Cleveland award of 1888, and the 1907 Washington treaties by which the Central American republics had conceded the use of their navigable waters to each other. El Salvador, speaking also for Honduras, argued that Nicaragua had no right to alienate the Gulf of Fonseca to an outside power, thus sacrificing the sovereignty of her sisters and exposing them to the risk of warlike actions, a reference to the European conflict then in progress. The implication of these protests was not wasted in Washington: if the United States encouraged Nicaragua's defiance, it would be morally responsible for the breakdown of the peace structure established in the 1907 treaties. Hoping to meet their objections, the United States Senate added an amendment to its ratification of the Bryan-Chamorro Treaty stating that nothing in that convention was intended "to affect any existing right" those countries might have.

Disappointed with this answer to their protests, Costa Rica and El Salvador appealed to the Central American Court of Justice. On September 30, 1916, and on March 2, 1917, the Costa Rican and Salvadorean governments won their cases, and the judges enjoined Nicaragua to correct the situation. Since the Court had no jurisdiction over the United States, however, the judges hesitated to declare the Bryan-Chamorro Treaty null and void, though that was in fact the practical effect of their decisions. Instead of obeying the Court, Nicaragua gave her year's notice of withdrawal from the Central American system established by the Washington treaties of 1907. The Court itself ceased to exist in March 1918 at the expiration of its ten-year authorization. Thus, Central America's peace machinery fell in a shambles.[23] No amount of legalistic reasoning can absolve the United States from responsibility for undermining the corner-stone of that system. Nicaragua was not a free agent, and all the parties concerned knew it.

Trying to make the best of a bad situation after the Court began to crumble, Costa Rica invited her sisters to attend a conference in San José, hoping to work out some measures for the collective security of Central America. Undoubtedly this 1917 attempt at union was based in a large part on resentment toward the United States. Like so many of its predecessors, however, the movement faltered because of diversionary tactics by the various state governments. El Salvador provoked a heated discussion when it suggested that the United States and Mexico should participate in the meeting, and Nicaragua agreed to participate only if Panama were invited, also suggesting that the impending conference be held either in Washington or in Panama. Honduras reminded Nicaragua that Central America was disunited enough without bringing in a country that had not been a member of the original federal pact; besides, Article 136 in the Panamanian constitution, permitting American intervention, deprived that country of its sovereignty. Considering the Yankeephobia generated by the recent controversy over the Bryan-Chamorro Treaty, the Nicaraguan proposals added to the frustrations of Central Americans and embittered them toward the Chamorro regime. At Versailles the head of the Honduran delegation, ex-president Policarpo Bonilla, made his famous statement on the Monroe Doctrine: that it should be multilateral, and that it should not prevent the confederation of states—an allusion to the recent failure of unionism, blaming the influence of the United States for the outcome.[24]

[23] Karnes, *op. cit.*, pp. 200-2.
[24] *Ibid.*, pp. 207-10.

After years of patient waiting and dedication to its ideals the *Partido Unionista* under Salvador Mendieta realized its golden opportunity as Guatemalans in all walks of life grew weary of the tyrant Estrada Cabrera—the continual spying of his agents, the mockery of democratic institutions, the corruption and graft, the enslavement of the poor Indians, the favoritism to foreigners, and the regime's anticlericalism and antilaborism. Linking reforms to their major objective of unionism, and displaying perfect discipline in their public demonstrations, Guatemalan unionists exploited and directed the mounting discontent against the dictator. On March 4, 1920, Estrada Cabrera's hand-picked congress passed a resolution favoring unionism; five weeks later it declared Estrada Cabrera insane, forcing his resignation, and Carlos Herrera, a prominent civilian, was chosen to rule in the interim. In the August elections, the first free ones in almost a century, Guatemalans chose Herrera as their president, committed to a program of reforms and Central American union.[25]

In December 1920 enthusiastic unionists from all over Central America gathered in San José, Costa Rica, to lay the groundwork for the area's fifth general government, which everyone hoped would be fully operative by September 15, 1921, the centennial of independence. According to form, Nicaraguans obstructed the proceedings by insisting on the acceptance of the Bryan-Chamorro Treaty; they walked out when the other delegations refused to compromise the sovereignty of their states. Representatives of four states signed the *pacto de unión* on January 19, 1921; Guatemala, Honduras, and El Salvador immediately ratified the agreement, thus implementing the dream of unionists everywhere. A provisional Federal Council was now the supreme authority of the land, at least as far as three states were concerned. In July 1921 a national constituent assembly met in Tegucigalpa to frame a document that would make *La Federación de Centro América* a republic worthy of Francisco Morazán's memory. The enthusiasm was electrifying. Liberals were in complete command: Mendieta was appointed to one of the secretaryships, and Policarpo Bonilla led the assembly.

Then the roof began to cave in as Costa Ricans, blaming everybody but themselves, voted against joining the general government. No

[25] *Ibid.*, pp. 211-12; Munro, *Intervention*, pp. 457-65.

sooner had the unionists recovered from this serious setback than they learned that on December 5, 1921, three *caudillos* had toppled the Herrera government in Guatemala—generals José María Orellana, Jorge Ubico, and José María Larrave, former supporters of Estrada Cabrera who apparently could not thrive in an atmosphere of freedom. Maintaining the fiction of favoring union, General Orellana sent a new delegation to Tegucigalpa. The Federal Council refused to recognize it. On the contrary, federal leaders, using the power granted to them by the *pacto*, ordered the governments of Honduras and El Salvador to restore by force the legitimate government of Guatemala. Before proceeding with this order, however, Policarpo Bonilla wisely suggested that the federal government first consult the United States.[26]

Although not intentionally antiunion, American actions could hardly be construed as favorable to Central American unity. Liberal unionists still resented the Bryan-Chamorro Treaty; there was no secret about this. American ships assumed threatening poses along the coasts of Central America wherever unionists gathered or important union decisions were being made, ill-advised maneuvers if their purpose was to protect American lives and property, for unionist demonstrations had been consistently well-disciplined. The *coup de grace*, however, was the reply Secretary of State Charles Evans Hughes gave the federal authorities: the United States would not sanction Central Americans' intervention in each other's affairs; the Central American nations should adhere to the Washington treaties of 1907. This last suggestion was indeed a remarkable one considering the significance of the Bryan-Chamorro Treaty.

That was all the Orellana government had to hear. On January 14, 1922, Guatemala assumed its complete sovereignty; the following month Guatemalans legalized Orellana's position as president, and within two months the United States recognized him, abandoning President Wilson's former policy of "constitutionalism" as a prerequisite for recognition. Apparently the rules changed with the circumstances as in Chatfield's day. Understandably, many Central American observers concluded that the United States had deliberately sabotaged the new union movement of Central America. Unable to

[26] Karnes, *op. cit.*, pp. 212-20.

enforce or implement its police powers, for this was the practical effect of Hughes' dictum, the Federation collapsed. By February 7, 1922, both Honduras and El Salvador had resumed their autonomy.[27]

In December the United States called its Central American charges to Washington and closely supervised their juridical labors. By February 7, 1923, a new Washington treaty and a host of conventions and protocols were completed and signed, establishing a new peace structure for Central America, only a pale reflection of its predecessor. The United States gained the right to appoint one of the six judges of the new Central American Tribunal, a body of limited jurisdiction; it could not, for example, judge issues affecting sovereignty. The United States, it would seem, wanted no further embarrassing discussion of the Bryan-Chamorro Treaty.

The second Washington treaty remained in effect until January 1, 1934, but its impact upon Central America was of little consequence. The relative peace of the 1920s was mainly the result of American intervention, however irritating the presence of United States' ships and marines may have been to Central America's liberals.

In Nicaragua the legation guard of marines was withdrawn in 1925 after a reasonably fair election in the previous fall that brought a coalition administration into office. An anti-Chamorro conservative, Carlos Solórzano, headed the ticket, and Juan Bautista Sacasa, a liberal, ran for the vice-presidency. But the United States' ex-ally Emiliano Chamorro could not leave well enough alone. In January 1926 he ousted the government and reimposed his will on the nation, much to the embarrassment of the State Department. Since the treaty of 1923 prohibited the recognition of illegal regimes, the United States placed Adolfo Díaz in charge of the government in November 1926, hoping that he would be an acceptable provisional executive until early 1929, when a newly elected government would assume office. But Sacasa, the ex-vice-president, would not consent to this compromise, and civil war broke out, with Sacasa receiving aid from the Mexican government. This brought on a second marine intervention to maintain the peace and supervise fair elections.

Not all liberals were willing to accept the American plan, and one of them, General Augusto César Sandino, entered Nicaragua's Val-

[27] Ibid., pp. 220-22. Munro, *Intervention*, pp. 465-68.

halla for his defiance of the United States and destruction of American property. Supported by the people, the famous *guerrillero* eluded the marines and the national guard, which American military advisors had trained. Only after Sacasa agreed to cooperate with the United States and the marines had left Nicaragua in January 1933 did Sandino put down his arms. On February 21, 1934, after dining with his old friend President Sacasa, Sandino was treacherously murdered by members of the national guard. When Sacasa tried to take steps to punish the assassins, the head of the national guard would not permit him to do so, thus implicating himself in the public eye. That young man was the nephew by marriage of President Sacasa—his name, General Anastacio Somoza.

And thus the United States' "big stick" policy in Central America came to an end. Sandino's popularity with Nicaraguans provides a fitting and sad commentary on that approach to the problems of Central America.

Continuismo (*1930s and 1940s*)

The economic underpinnings of Central America, which began to buckle in the 1890s, were further weakened by the downswing of coffee prices before World War I. Bananas and other commodities took up the slack somewhat but never enough to put the countries on a firm footing, especially as natural catastrophes, like the earthquake of 1917 in Guatemala, and diseases hit the major crops. The dislocations in world trade during World War I increased the dependence of Central American countries upon the United States as a market and as a source of credit. As long as prosperity reigned in the North, financial assistance from the United States tended to cover over the weaknesses in the Central American economies and lulled their leaders into a sense of complacency. Only in Costa Rica, during the liberal administration of Ricardo Jiménez Oreamuno from 1924 to 1928, was there an effort to relieve the drain on foreign exchange by taking over some of the functions of insurance companies.

Then came the crash of 1929. Coffee prices plummeted to new lows, and everybody felt the pinch. With profits virtually nonexistent, producers had no choice but to lay off workers and to lower wages, further depressing labor's standard of living. The unemployed, leaving the cities and going back home, in turn strained food supplies in the subsistence sector of the economy. And there was not much that the governments could do now that customs receipts were down and loans were hard to get from the United States. Brazil's futile efforts to stabilize coffee prices in the 1930s helped Central American growers slightly without solving the real problem of overspecialization. The same was true of New Deal measures—the reciprocal trade program and the Export-Import loans. It took World War II, with its demand for products the enemy controlled in the Far East, to bring about a greater diversification of Central America's economy.

In the meantime there were rumblings of discontent among the masses of Central America, no longer willing to accept complacently the do-nothing policies of their political masters. They wanted food, housing, and land, not empty slogans. And a new generation of leaders, some from the middle classes and some from the ranks of labor, assured them that these things were possible by following a program of economic nationalism. In Costa Rica, for example, the Communist party made considerable headway in political circles from the beginning of the Great Depression, electing two deputies to Congress by 1934. It also organized the banana workers in the Limón district and got minimum wage provisions for them. Recognizing that new forces were abroad in the land, President Jiménez made a number of concessions during his last term from 1932 to 1936. Moreover, he organized the National Republican party in 1932 on a permanent basis, committed to a program of minimum wage legislation, social security, a labor code, and so forth, and the party succeeded in winning subsequent elections.[28] These reforms and the manner in which they were made perhaps did not satisfy the followers of José Figueres, but they were at least steps in the right direction, which is more than can be said for what was going on in other countries of Central America. In the process, Costa Ricans were at least maintaining some semblance of democratic institutions.

Elsewhere in Central America four colorful strongmen came to the fore, overwhelming their countrymen in behalf of the *status quo*, like the *caudillos* of old. For 13 years General Maximiliano Hernández

[28] Franklin D. Parker, *The Central American Republics* (London, 1964), pp. 263-64.

Martínez (1931-44) made his Salvadorean followers cower under the brute strength of the military, when he was not holding them spellbound with crackpot divinations. No less imposing was General Tiburcio Carías Andino (1933-49), an ex-liberal who championed the conservative cause in Honduras with the fanaticism of a convert and the precision of a military expert. General Jorge Ubico (1931-44) ruled Guatemala with the same exploitive instincts he had displayed under Estrada Cabrera as Retalhuleu's *jefe político*, and General Anastacio Somoza (1936-56) applied his bookkeeping talents and military "persuasion" to develop what contemporary Nicaraguans call "Somoza, S.A."—*Sociedad Anónima* being the equivalent of *Inc*. The fact that they all had much in common—the first two, conservatives, and the last two, liberals—aptly illustrates what had happened to Barrio's "new liberalism" over the course of seven decades.

As dictators, they centralized government much more than their predecessors had been able to do, and in this sense, their regimes provided a nationalistic foundation for future governments. They accomplished this centralization by various means: the control of a modernized military organization with new weapons that made dissidents think twice before challenging them; press censorship and the use of government spies to "encourage" mass conformity to governmental programs; the exile or imprisonment of the opposition, oftentimes liquidated while "trying to escape," as the official reports read; and "exemplary punishment," like the Salvadorean bloodbath of 1932 in which thousands of poverty-stricken Indians were wiped out because Hernández thought that they had joined a Communist plot to take over the government. The ball-and-chain prisoners working in the streets of Tegucigalpa was Carías' answer to crime and political opposition. The liberal dictators were only a bit more sophisticated.

Despite constitutional restrictions the four dictators mastered the process of *continuismo* by the historic expedient of changing the constitution. Hernández got a new constitution in 1939, and a term extension in February 1944 that permitted him to rule until 1949; Carías pushed through the constitution of 1936, amended in 1939, which allowed him to continue in office until 1949; Somoza, as a liberal, felt the need for more constitutional hocus-pocus—the constitutions of 1939, 1948, 1950, and the amendment of 1955; Ubico's congress, also preoccupied with consistency, merely "suspended" the no-re-election clause of Barrios' constitution in 1935 and 1941. In the meantime the congressional and judicial branches of government came more and more under the control of the executive. Moreover, in Guatemala and Honduras the municipalities became mere creatures of the central government, losing the prerogatives they had reassumed since Barrios' time.

In meeting the problems of the depression the conservative dictators displayed little imagination. Hernández tried to "defend" coffee prices by the 1933 law; the coffee growers, comprised mainly of the local "families," welcomed this intervention, at the same time resisting any social reforms. Hernández, moreover, did not try to diversify the economy to any great extent. Cotton growing was a result of war demands, not of any conscious governmental measure. In Honduras, Carías' cure for the depression was limited to helping the banana companies by resisting labor unions and balancing the budget. He cut the salaries of bureaucrats and did bring financial order to Honduras, though the construction of schools and other public projects had to be sacrificed in the process. Coffee growing in Honduras was a postwar development. In short, Hernández and Carías merely held the line, except in distributing political spoils. Nepotism and favoritism characterized their regimes.

On the other hand, in economic matters the liberal dictators followed Barrios' brand of positivism somewhat more closely. Although Somoza was financially a conservative, he at least tried to encourage the diversification of Nicaragua's economy by establishing confidence in it and inviting foreign investors to consider new fields. Thus he prepared Nicaragua for her economic renaissance in the post-World War II period. Labor did not flourish under Somoza, but he did recognize the theoretical existence of the workingman's rights, which was more than his liberal cohort in Guatemala was willing to do.

Ubico's government was only a step above its conservative neighbors. Although the "Iron Dictator" pushed economic measures with greater vigor than they did, he nevertheless held the line by supporting the established coffee and banana industries controlled by foreign companies. Antilaborism, low wages, and minimum land taxes were the incentives his government provided Guatemalan landowners, and his cooperation with American interests won him special concessions for Guatemalan coffee in the U.S. market. At times this cooperation worked against the best interest of his country. He supported, for example, UFCO's move in 1936 to buy the controlling share of IRCA, the International Railways of Central America, which led to discriminatory rates against competitors on the Pacific coast. And he also permitted UFCO to renege on its promise to build effective port installations on the Pacific, an act that nullified Barrios' nationalistic objectives.

Much of the progress that took place under Ubico, moreover, was made at the expense of the defenseless Indian. A presidential decree of 1933 compelled Indian males to work two weeks annually without pay on highway construction if they could not meet the exemption tax of two *pesos*. According to the testimony of contemporaries, unscrupulous government officials victimized the Indian with impunity, taking his money and forcing him to work anyway. Those who complained ended in jail.

Apologists of Ubico—and there are many of them—point out the dictator's humanitarianism in helping the Indian by ending debt peonage in 1934. Less literal-minded, the natives wished that their *ladino* masters had not been so charitable, for in removing one evil they had replaced it with another one still worse—the vagrancy law of the same year. According to this piece of legislation, *all* Indians, not just those who had been in debt, had to work at least 150 days a year. The employers registered the days worked in a special booklet which the Indians had to carry with them.[29] This particular law was rigidly enforced, since it guaranteed cheap, forced labor. The potential for abuse was unlimited. *Ladinos* might live poorly because of depressed economic conditions, but they at least had the Indians to give them a sense of superiority and to do their menial tasks. Perhaps that is why *Ubiquismo* (peace, order, and honest government) still has so many adherents in modern-day Guatemala. Let us hope that Peralta's "Operation Honesty" will be more faithful to its alleged principles than its Ubican predecessor.

As World War II loomed on the horizon, Central Americans

[29] Nathan L. Whetten, *Guatemala: The Land and the People* (New Haven, 1961), pp. 119-22.

seemed no better off than they had been in the days of Justo Rufino Barrios. Seventy years of "progress" had merely perpetuated the old social order with new partners, erasing the former ideological cleavage between liberals and conservatives. Yet the seedlings of discontent were pushing upward, ready to unseat the *caudillos* at the first opportunity.

FOUR

LEGACY OF WAR

1944-1954

The [Guatemalan] revolution was not without
justification. But the Communists seized on it,
not as an opportunity for real reform, but as a
chance to gain political power.[1]

John Foster Dulles, June 30, 1954

With their raw materials and foodstuffs, Central Americans helped the Allied war effort against the Axis and in the process
gained important benefits. Cut off from former suppliers, they were
forced to develop infant industries, and the demands of war further
diversified their economy with new agricultural commodities and
minerals. Rising prices stimulated the region's economic life, revers-
ing the former deflationary trend and causing labor and the salaried
middle class to demand a higher share of the national income. Moreover, the association with the world's democracies undermined Central America's dictators, two of whom fell before the war's end. Only
Somoza survived the onslaught of democratic forces, perhaps because
his regime displayed more imagination. Political unionism also re-
surged in the immediate postwar years, though it eventually gave
way to an emphasis on economic cooperation as a result of intraregional disputes and domestic problems.

[1] United States Department of State, *Intervention of International Communism
in Guatemala* (Washington, 1954), p. 30.

For a few years it appeared that Guatemala and Honduras might sustain the democratic upsurge, just as Costa Rica did, but international factors came into play. In Guatemala, Communists capitalized upon ultranationalism to twist the objectives of the 1944 "Revolution" to their own advantage, thus alienating the loyalty of many one-time supporters of that movement and weakening the control of moderates. In addition, the hostility of American interests forced the downfall of a regime that was nothing more than a military despotism in its final months. That fateful intervention has vitally affected United States' policy in Latin America ever since.

Fall of the Tyrants

As the European conflict came to an end, discontent was rampant throughout Central America. The people were no longer willing to condone the arbitrary and anachronistic governments of the *caudillos.* Since 1942 unionist leaders had revived their crusade for effective democratic institutions and much-needed reforms, and their propaganda found a sounding board throughout Central America.

In the winter of 1943-44 Salvadoreans in all walks of life were insulted by the dictator's brutal reprisals against the opposition and bald attempt to perpetuate his rule by calling a new constituent assembly for February 1944. In April the nation rebelled, and the general strike compelled Hernández Martínez to resign on May 8th. For the next four years the dictator clung to his hope of making a comeback as provisional governments struggled for stability without yielding to reformist pressures. General Salvador Castañeda Castro dominated the interim period and was finally ousted by a faction of reform-conscious military men. After 18 months of junta rule Colonel Oscar Osorio led his country into the 1950s—a story we have already told.

The Guatemalan pattern was similar. Discontent was especially evident in the major urban centers among students, lawyers, artisans, teachers, and businessmen; in short, the articulate segments of Guatemalan society were disposed to give up their support of the tyrant. On June 22, 1944, Ubico suspended personal guarantees; two days later there were public readings of the Atlantic Charter, accompanied by demands that the dictator resign. It almost seemed that history was repeating itself—the events of 1920 all over again. On the 29th Ubico resigned, leaving his friend General Federico Ponce to guard the keys to the prison he had built over the years. But Ponce was unable to hold back the "Revolution," and on October 20, 1944, a glorious day in the minds of many Guatemalans, a military triumvirate deposed him and prepared the nation for a new constitutional regime, which was duly established on March 15, 1945.

In Honduras, Tiburcio Carías Andino weathered the storm a few years longer and decided to bow out gracefully by permitting presidential elections in October 1948. On New Year's Day, Carías' choice took over the executive's chair. Few suspected that Dr. Juan Manuel Gálvez would be anything more than a puppet for his old boss. Yet Gálvez did have ideas of his own, and during the next five years, some say, he accomplished more than his predecessor had in 15. To be sure, the record of material accomplishments was substantial, following the recommendations of foreign experts that Honduras diversify her economy and build a good road system. Foreign investors responded generously and with confidence to the incentives offered by Gálvez' government, and the Honduran economy picked up momentum. It was during this period that coffee became a prominent export, relieving the nation's dependence upon bananas. The cattle industry also thrived.

But Gálvez did more than stimulate Honduras' dormant economy. The number of schools constructed during his administration and the health measures adopted illustrated his concern for a modern Honduras. A firm believer in constitutional government, Gálvez also prepared his people for elections in the fall of 1954. Itching to get back in office, Carías Andino actively sought and gained the nomination of the National party, a move that antagonized the anti-*personalistas* of the party, who proceeded to nominate their own candidate. This division in the government's ranks in turn gave the Liberal party an advantage, and they exploited the opportunity to the utmost. Gálvez' commitment to the downfall of Arbenz, and the government's actions during the major strike of 1954, further enhanced the candidacy of Ramón Villeda Morales. He won the most votes in that election, though he was not permitted to assume the presidency until 1957, for reasons which have already been discussed in Chapter One. Carías' poor showing in the elections was a graphic reminder that Hondurans had outgrown their *caudillo*.

From April to July 1954, a new force disturbed the Honduran scene, one that could no longer be ignored—the labor movement. Carías and Gálvez had shackled labor as an incentive to private enterprise. The fruits of that disastrous policy were evident in the crippling strike of 1954.[2] The fact that foreign companies were involved, UFCO in particular, added the explosive issue of nationalism, especially when those companies resorted to strikebreaking tactics long since outmoded in the United States. The reaction of Honduran labor—not just banana workers—was spontaneous, unorganized, and violent, an expression of the workingman's long-standing and deep resentment toward those who had callously ignored him for decades and prevented him from organizing because he was considered a mere commodity, not a human being. Honduran Communists and their Guatemalan collaborators had nothing to do with the initial demonstrations, though, of course, they soon tried to capture the movement for their own purposes. It should be noted, however, that non-Communist labor leaders gained control of the strike and made the final settlement, thanks to the cooperation of hemispheric labor organizations.

The last of the quartet, Anastacio Somoza, proved to be more flexible and enlightened in economic matters. As far as political democracy was concerned, his stripes never changed, though occasionally he made formal gestures in that direction, perhaps to satisfy a foreign audience; the practice was something else again. Undoubtedly his economic record could not have been possible without Nicaragua's bountiful resources and fertile land. Yet it is to his credit that he purposively developed those assets and created the proper conditions for national development—a road system, port facilities, public health, schools, labor code, social security, and so forth. To be sure, the labor movement he encouraged during World War II was a captive one, but it at least prevented a violent explosion of the type that shook Honduras.

[2] For an excellent discussion of this strike see John D. Martz, *Central America: The Crisis and the Challenge* (Chapel Hill, 1959), pp. 130-41.

Somoza's country in the 1950s had the most flourishing economy in Central America; this is a matter of record. And much of this was due to the fact that the dictator faithfully implemented the suggestions that had been made by a special mission of the International Bank. Moreover, on various occasions Somoza demonstrated an awareness of the weakness inherent in monoculture and deliberately strove to balance the economy by encouraging agricultural diversification and industrial development. It is true that Somoza and his family benefited most from these materialistic accomplishments, but this should not detract from the impact of his measures upon the national structure.

An assassin felled the Nicaraguan strongman on September 21, 1956, and Somoza died a week later. Yet his regime, as we noted in Chapter One, still lives on, a phenomenon attributable largely to the old dictator's imaginative policies in economic and social matters. Anastacio Somoza and Justo Rufino Barrios had a great deal in common.

Spiritual Socialism (1945-1951)

A huge and imposing figure, Juan José Arévalo was the popular choice of the amorphous elements that forced Ubico's resignation and resisted Ponce's attempt to perpetuate military rule in Guatemala during the momentous events of October 1944. As an intellectual whose writings on education, philosophy, and politics had attracted wide attention in Guatemala and throughout Latin America, Arévalo was the logical preference of students and professionals who had headed the anti-Ubico demonstrations. His ideas on Central American unionism were especially popular. Arévalo's middle class origins, the fact that he was a civilian who had lived as an exile in Argentina rather than work for the fallen dictator, his nationalistic fervor, and his commitment to social and economic reforms attracted still others to his banner. Moreover, just 40, he represented the type of leader that youth wanted and an older generation could respect. In December he polled 85 per cent of the vote in a fair election and became president on March 15, 1945, for a six-year term. On that same day a new constitution was promulgated.

In the campaign, in his inaugural address, and in subsequent speeches President Arévalo increased his popularity as he tried to give the "Guatemalan Revolution" its ideological bearing, the mystical and somewhat nebulous doctrine of "spiritual socialism." Actually there was nothing new in this doctrine, if it can indeed be called that; the noted Argentine liberal of the first half of the nineteenth century, Esteban Echeverría, had expounded on this subject in his classic study *El Dogma Socialista,* nor had it been original with Echeverría. In short, Arévalo advocated a program of "constructive liberalism," along the lines we discussed in Chapter One in regard to José Figueres in Costa Rica. Yet it is interesting, as well as significant, that Arévalo chose not to call his doctrine "liberalism," precisely because that term had been discredited and distorted in Guatemala by the likes of Ubico and Estrada Cabrera.

In true nineteenth-century fashion, Arévalo emphasized the word *dignidad,* not only of the individual but of the nation. Against the other "socialisms"—communism, nazism, fascism, and he might have added "positivism" as it was described in the last chapter—which made man a mere cog in a machine, Arévalo wanted to preserve the individual's spiritual nature, dignity, and noble qualities. Such an individual would be psychologically committed and linked to the collective whole—the enlightened nation of Guatemala. And this Guatemalan nationalism would not be chauvinistic and selfish; it would be a humanitarian nationalism. His insistence that foreign nations and their subjects respect Guatemala's sovereignty and dignity likewise had historical roots. Guatemalans understood the context well and were not frightened by the word *socialism,* as used by Arévalo. On the contrary, they welcomed it; apparently they still do.

In the practical field of politics, "spiritual socialism" became known as "Arevalismo." Although some observers claim that there was a difference between the two, Arévalo never made such a distinction. And he was fully justified: one was the *mystique,* and the other was a program of action, conditioned and influenced by political realities. Political expediency—pragmatism, if you will—should not detract from Arévalo's total contribution to modern Guatemala. His record of achievement in six years was remarkable by any standards, and that imprint has been permanent and inerasable.

The constitution of March 15, 1945, derived from many sources.[3] The natural law provisions, the emphasis upon legislative supremacy, the safeguards against executive misrule, and the insistence upon an apolitical military force represented traditional liberal aspirations. So was the penchant for municipal autonomy, freedom for political parties, the secret ballot, and compulsory voting of all literate males. For illiterate males the vote was optional and public; illiterate females could not vote, and for the literate variety the vote was optional and secret. Since Indians constituted the bulk of the population, this was clearly an attempt to integrate them into the national system—that is, to further the process of ladinoization. The Indians' response to this and other reforms was enthusiastic: finally, here was a government that genuinely had their interests at heart. And as they began to participate in politics, they inevitably challenged the traditional social structure. Young leaders replaced the *principales* of the old cultural hierarchy, and *ladino* politicians had to woo their Indian constituents, not just take them for granted.

As an educator, it is not surprising that President Arévalo should take great interest in conquering illiteracy, for as long as that problem existed, national progress would always be slow. Schools were constructed. Cultural missions tried, without too much success, to bring education to the Indians. Later, special educational centers for peasants were established, and in 1946 the *Instituto Indigenista Nacional* was founded to coordinate the activities of these *nucleos escolares campesinos*. The *Instituto* was also a research center that studied linguistics, conducted surveys on problems of native rural life, and even worked out credit facilities for self-sufficient small farmers. The education and acculturation of the Indian had many facets, and the *Instituto* did a commendable job. The idea was not to force the white man's way of life on the Indian but rather to facilitate the Indian's entry into national life, bringing into it his own rich heritage. The end product would be a Guatemalan with distinctive features. And finally, the constitution of 1945 authorized the Universidad de San Carlos to resume its autonomy, which Barrios had taken away from it.

[3] See the penetrating analysis of Kalman H. Silvert, A *Study in Government: Guatemala* (New Orleans, 1954), pp. 13-18.

The Arévalo government introduced long-needed social and labor reforms, implementing the constitutional mandate to bring Guatemala abreast with the modern world in these matters. Established in 1946, the *Instituto Guatemalteco de Seguridad Social* (IGSS) provided, as it does today, social security and medical coverage for Guatemalan workers. The imposing Roosevelt Hospital, a project outlined during the Ubico regime and largely financed by the United States, was opened under Arévalo. Public health institutions, despite limited finances, inadequate staffs, and formidable obstacles, struggled to raise standards of hygiene and sanitation, and with the support of the Pan American Health Organization, INCAP opened its doors in 1949 to study and improve nutrition throughout Central America and Panama. Moreover, the labor code of 1947 made possible the unionization of industrial and agrarian workers, providing labor courts for the settlement of work disputes and benefits and safeguards for the workingman. Since labor had been straitjacketed by all previous governments, it is understandable that union leaders were aggressive and that Communists found a fertile field in which to operate.

As might be expected, the development of a modern and well-balanced economy was a major objective of Arévalo's administration. The industrial development law of November 1947 contained incentives for new industries, and foreign investors were invited to participate in the process on the same terms as nationals. By June 1950, 78 industries had obtained concessions under this law. The *Compañía Minería de Guatemala*, fully owned by United States citizens who were interested in exploiting the lead resources of the country was the type of foreign company that was welcomed during the Arévalo regime.[4]

Although Arévalo appreciated the need for agrarian reform, his preoccupation with other revolutionary measures prevented him from doing much about it. Considering the power of the landowners, he perhaps felt that it was wise to proceed indirectly even though the Constitution specifically prohibited *latifundia* and empowered the government to expropriate private property in the public interest after

[4] A basic reference for economic matters during the Arévalo period is the report of the International Bank for Reconstruction and Development, *The Economic Development of Guatemala* (Baltimore, 1952).

indemnifying its owners. The right to form agricultural unions helped the laborer against his *finquero*, and the law of forced rental was intended to prevent smaller landholders from exploiting their tenant farmers by keeping rental payments low.[5] The land law of 1949, moreover, made it possible for landless persons to rent two acres by applying to the government; the lands in question were the *Fincas Nacionales* confiscated from Germans during World War II at the request of the United States.

The problems Arévalo faced in implementing these various reforms were indeed formidable, and it is to his credit that he succeeded as well as he did. The lack of trained administrators to staff the various autonomous agencies that carried out the reform measures and administered governmental interests was a serious problem in the early days of Arévalo's tenure, for it took time and money to train competent experts. Perhaps the most crucial obstacle was the lack of money to implement the programs on a large scale. To have imposed heavy taxes on people who were accustomed to not paying taxes would certainly have invited even more resistance than Arévalo encountered during his six years as president. As it was, he admitted to 17 uprisings against him; others claim that double that figure is closer to the truth.[6] And much of the money that should have gone into the reform program had to be used just to keep Arévalo in office, and in the process, of course, the democratic features of the constitution had to be suspended.

Inaugurated in 1946, the *Banco de Guatemala*, a financial reform in itself, had as its objectives the stabilization of exchange and the stimulation of credit for productive activities. At first, war earnings helped to supply resources for governmental projects, but by 1947 it had become increasingly difficult for the government to make ends meet. The internal debt by then was five million *quetzales*; three years later it had tripled, and the government turned, more and more, to deficit spending.[7] International bankers, moreover, did not wish to lend money to a government they thought hostile to foreign com-

---

[5] Richard N. Adams, *Cultural Surveys of Panama-Nicaragua-Guatemala-El Salvador-Honduras* (Washington, D.C., 1957), pp. 297-98.

[6] Silvert, *op. cit.*, p. 16.

[7] *Ibid.*, p. 36

panies—the UFCO case, which we shall discuss below. Lacking domestic venture capital, Arévalo organized the *Instituto de Fomento de la Producción* in 1948 to capitalize economic development with government funds. Although initially a financing agency, INFOP has also served as a development corporation that conducts surveys of the economy, makes plans for future development projects, and manages governmental interests in numerous economic activities. Like the IGSS in the field of social security, INFOP is an autonomous organization and therefore less susceptible to political pressures or changes. It welcomes private enterprise to collaborate with government in advancing the national economy, a significant and lasting reform.

By our standards, Arévalo's reform program was moderate and certainly would be welcomed under the present Alliance for Progress. But considering Guatemala's past, it constituted a real revolution, and the vested interests of the old order did not submit gracefully to an experiment of modernization that threatened their way of life. The weakening of Arévalo's former support, quite evident in the proliferation of parties in the late 1940s, suggests also that many of his ex-followers were not genuinely interested in facing the consequences and implications of modernization. Perhaps the "Revolution" had already gone too far; higher wages for labor meant higher prices for goods, and a household could not be operated as cheaply as before.

It would seem that the crucial turning point of the Arévalo administration came in late 1947, when UFCO's workers at Tiquisate, the western division, demanded a basic wage of 1.50 *quetzales* a day, along with certain fringe benefits. Within a year's time nationalistic feeling in Guatemala had reached a fever pitch because of UFCO's reaction to labor leaders who were experiencing the headiness of newly won power. After an illegal strike on July 1, 1948, the company retaliated by a one-day shutdown at Tiquisate. A labor judge secured a temporary truce, but in December the company refused to obey an executive order to resume arbitration after trouble had broken out at Puerto Barrios and at Bananera, the eastern division, idling workers in both locations and seriously affecting the industries that depended upon imported raw materials. UFCO's defiance of the executive order raised the explosive nationalistic issue—a foreign company considering itself above the law and showing no respect for Guatemala's sovereignty. The next step was even more provocative. UFCO took its case to the floor of the United States Congress, where Senator Henry Cabot Lodge averred that Arévalo was "Communistically inclined." [8] The situation calmed down in 1949, and UFCO signed a one-year contract starting on March 5. But the damage had already been done, paving the way for further acrimonious relations between Arbenz and the American company.

The issue of "imperialism" embarrassed the middle-of-the-road position of President Arévalo and at the same time strengthened the extremists in Guatemala. In 1948 the reactionary Right formed the *Partido de Unificación Anticomunista* (PUA), which opposed all the objectives of the "Revolution" and hoped that the U.S. marines would help them turn back the clock in their country. North American businessmen and a few high military men were sympathetic to the negativistic stance of the *Puistas*, admirers of an authoritarian Church and the rule of the landed oligarchy. In the eyes of *Puistas*, Arévalo was a Communist, and everything his government did to modernize Guatemala was Communistic. Knowing that they could never win at the polls, the *Puistas* were forever threatening military action—threats that were frequently implemented, it might be added. As the elections of 1950 approached, many rightists were backing the candidacy of General Francisco Javier Arana, the chief of staff under Arévalo and a member of the triumvirate that had deposed Ponce in October 1944. In early 1948 Arana informally announced his intentions to run for the presidency.[9]

At the other extreme, the militant Left was pressuring Arévalo to take a stronger stand against foreign interests and the rightists, feeling that his compromise tactics were sacrificing unduly the interests of Guatemala. As might be expected, Communists exploited the deep-seated resentment of Guatemalans toward the United States and suggested to the ultranationalists that Arévalo had to change his ways, including his unsympathetic policy toward Communists. In 1944 the Communists had been few in number, but thereafter

[8] Archer C. Bush, *Organized Labor in Guatemala, 1944-1949* (Hamilton, 1950), p. 25.
[9] Silvert, *op. cit.*, pp. 54-56.

they became increasingly important, as well as useful, because of their zeal and willingness to work toward social and economic reforms. Compensating for the inexperience of Guatemalan labor, they provided the leadership for the major unions. Victor Manuel Gutiérrez was especially prominent in labor circles, while José Manuel Fortuny, his rival for the top spot in the party, preferred to operate within the *Partido de Acción Revolucionaria* (PAR), the principal governmental organ, which was formed in late 1945.

Fearful of a Communist take-over, and perhaps guided by the mistakes of the Spanish Civil War, President Arévalo invoked Article 32 of the constitution, which prohibited parties of an international nature. On many occasions, moreover, he expressed his views concerning the impracticability of Communist ideas. In 1946 he suppressed the *Escuela Claridad*, a Marxist school that was indoctrinating young Guatemalans and among whose early graduates were Fortuny and Gutiérrez. In 1947 he banished some Communists for creating disturbances in rural areas. In that same year the party began to perfect its secret organization. Prior to the 1950 elections Arévalo again tried to dissociate known Communists from his administration, but by then they felt strong enough to come out into the open, thanks to the implicit support of another aspirant to the presidency, Jacobo Arbenz, the youthful minister of defense who had also served on the triumvirate that succeeded Ponce. Whether because of strong nationalistic sentiment or political ambition, Colonel Arbenz headed the faction in the Arévalo government that favored utilizing the Communists in carrying out the Guatemalan "Revolution." Perhaps the example of Perón was foremost in his mind. At any rate, his group undermined Arévalo's efforts to thwart the spread of Communist influence in Guatemala.

In the final analysis, it was the actions of extremists that forged the course of events in Guatemala, and moderates like Arévalo and the vast majority of his countrymen found themselves with limited alternatives, the black or the white. As Guatemalans they had no choice but to follow their nationalistic aspirations, though they would have preferred a more sensible approach. Some observers have blamed Arévalo for permitting the growth of Communist influence in the labor movement, naïvely assuming that Guatemala's labor history should have followed a different path than that experienced by other underdeveloped countries. Moreover, these same observers have accepted uncritically the facile "conspiratorial" interpretation of Guatemalan history: step by step the international conspirators led their nationalistic dupes down the primrose path. But this interpretation is like a horse with blinders; it blandly overlooks the conditions that gave the Communists an issue to exploit—the nationalistic issue raised by UFCO's defiance of and undisguised hostility to the Guatemalan "Revolution," not to mention the ideological implications of the *Puistas'* obstructionism. The Communists did not invent these things; they merely capitalized on them for their own advantage. In ladling out responsibility for subsequent events, it would seem more realistic to study the contribution of those elements that brought these issues to a head. Furthermore, we miss the significance of the Guatemalan "Revolution" if we start from the assumption that nationalism was not, or should not have been, a factor in that moment of crisis. It was, and this psychological phenomenon helps to explain the failure of the moderate approach Arévalo represented.

There is, however, one serious blot in Arévalo's record that has not yet been satisfactorily explained—the assassination of General Francisco Arana on July 18, 1949, just outside of Amatitlán, thereby eliminating a popular candidate for the presidency. Although not conclusive, the available evidence tends to implicate Colonel Arbenz, Arana's rival for control of the armed forces. What incriminates Arévalo is his failure to conduct a thorough investigation of the crime. He was unquestionably a "captive" of the Arbenz forces by this time, but that is hardly a justification for his inability to act on the matter. By glossing over the incident, he assumed some responsibility for it. The Right, it will be recalled, has not forgiven him.

From that time forward Arbenz' star was in the ascendant. He was the undisputed master of the military, and Arévalo seemed powerless to ignore his counsel. The Communists also benefited from the coup and brazenly came into the open by mid-1950, prior to the elections. And although Colonel Arbenz publicly disclaimed their support, it was common knowledge that he welcomed it. In the elections he polled 65 per cent of the vote, and on March 15,

1951, the 37-year-old military officer from Quezaltenango took over the presidency of his country. The militant Left was in charge of the situation, and Arévalo was conveniently sent out of the country on a diplomatic assignment. "Spiritual socialism" now gave way to the more mundane type.

Central American Unionism

In 1942 Central American unionists met in San José, where they outlined and committed themselves to an ambitious program of political reform, warning the four tyrants that the days of *continuismo* were limited.[10] Students and lawyers were especially prominent in this union movement, which in April, 1944, after the fall of Hernández Martínez, took on the name of *Unión Patriótica Centro-Americana*, a merger of Salvadorean and Guatemalan enthusiasts. In September they held a convention to discuss ways and means of forging an effective Central American union and formally proclaimed their support of Juan José Arévalo for the presidency of Guatemala. He was known to them because of a radio speech he had delivered in 1939 entitled "Culture and Cultural Possibilities in Central America," which extolled the region's cultural elements and advocated its unity, a greater nationalism for Central Americans to follow.[11] The Guatemalan constitution reflected the influence of unionists, in the clause on antimilitarism as well as in the mention of the desirability of union in the preamble and in other sections of the document. As in 1920, there was a feeling of urgency concerning the political and economic union of Central America.

Soon after his inauguration, and following the wishes of his unionist supporters, President Arévalo traveled to Santa Ana, El Salvador, where he conferred with President Salvador Castañeda Castro, who was also committed to the political and economic union of the two countries. Both hoped that their example would promote the adherence of other Central American countries. At the Santa Ana meeting the two leaders discussed the prospective merger and paved the

[10] Thomas L. Karnes, *The Failure of Union: Central America, 1824-1960* (Chapel Hill, 1959), pp. 231-32.
[11] Juan José Arévalo, "Cultura y posibilidades de cultura en América Central," *Escritos Políticos* (Guatemala, 1945), pp. 59-69.

way for it by declaring an open border and eliminating immigration barriers. They also considered the possibility of a combined banking system. In May they met again at San Cristóbal in El Salvador, where they agreed to set up a federal council in Santa Ana, consisting of six members, and to demonstrate their seriousness of purpose Guatemala and El Salvador formally announced their political merger to the United Nations in June, 1945, as unionists throughout Central America rejoiced. On September 15, 1946, the 125th anniversary of Central American independence, a federal constituent assembly opened its sessions. Among the committees formed by the delegates was the Junta of National Planning, an entity responsible for the promotion of industrial projects, the development of communications, and the improvement of electrical facilities. Its goal was to coordinate the economic life of the new Federal Republic, anticipating the present common market organization.

But the new federal government suffered the fate of its predecessors. Carías Andino of Honduras, fearing the democratic orientation of the two unionist states, hoped that Somoza of Nicaragua would join him in a counter bloc, but Somoza demurred, though it was obvious that he had no intentions of taking the federal experiment seriously. Following an established pattern, Costa Rica, under President Teodoro Picado, praised the project but stalled for time, claiming that she would hold a plebiscite to ascertain the will of her people. It was never held. In the meantime domestic problems distracted the two unionist partners, so that by 1947 it was clear that political union had again failed. Sensing that this was true, a group of Salvadorean and Guatemalan lawyers met in January of that year and agreed that they should satisfy themselves with moderate progress toward union. Thus, they drew up a new *Pacto* calling for a five-year transition period before establishing a firmer union. This would give them time to win mass support for their cause.[12] From this time forward, unionists placed their emphasis on economic cooperation, thus leading to the formation of ODECA in 1951 and the modern *Mercomún* of Central America, which we have already discussed in Chapter One.

[12] Karnes, *op. cit.*, pp. 233-34; Alberto Herrarte, *La unión de Centro América: Tragedia y esperanza* (Guatemala, 1955), pp. 287-91.

Considering the historical pattern of failure, the more immediate preoccupation with social and economic reforms, and the ubiquitous rivalry of the Central American states, this was a wise decision. Arévalo's troubles of the late forties made him turn, more and more, toward the Guatemalan scene alone, and although Arbenz started his administration by appointing Manuel Galich, a fervent unionist, to head the Ministry of Foreign Affairs, he was more interested in the national objectives of his own country. The fall of Castañeda in 1948 created a similar situation in El Salvador; Osorio put Salvadorean nationalism in first place, though he too was a unionist in the same sense as Arbenz. In 1948 the Costa Rican revolution occurred, revealing a basic ideological cleavage that would inevitably obstruct unionism in Central America: Somoza and Carías Andino aided the *Calderonistas*, while Arévalo demonstrated his sympathy for José Figueres. It is inconceivable that a Figueres and a Somoza could ever sit together at the same table without firing their .45's at each other; indeed, the record of Costa Rican-Nicaraguan relations from 1948 to 1956 provides more than sufficient proof of this contention. The arming of *emigrados*, the constant meddling in each other's affairs, the carnival-like challenges of two deadly enemies, and the assassination plots and rumors indicated that political progress in Central America was far from reaching the sophisticated level that effective union would require.[13]

In April 1953 odeca's promising start along the road to economic cooperation was threatened by the news that Salvadorean Foreign Minister Roberto Canessa would introduce a resolution at the next meeting denouncing international communism in Central America. Arbenz let it be known to Osorio that such an act would jeopardize odeca's continued existence. When the warning went unheeded, Guatemala withdrew from the regional organization and did not return until Castillo Armas came to power.

The Arbenz Era (1951-1954)

Guatemala's second revolutionary president was a young military officer who had compiled an impressive record at the *Escuela Politécnica* as a student, as an instructor, and as director. To the public

[13] For the details of the Figueres-Somoza rivalry see Martz, *op. cit.*, pp. 181-97.

he was an enigma: his speeches were delivered unemotionally, he had a reputation for being "tough" and ruthless in carrying out measures he believed to be right, and he appeared to be an introvert who harbored many strong feelings, including a resentment toward Guatemala's upper classes. Perhaps this was due to the social discrimination practiced in Guatemala City against military men and especially those coming from the highlands, the so-called *chivos*. The son of a Swiss druggist who committed suicide, Arbenz spent a lonely adolescence, living first with one relative and then another. He married a highly placed Salvadorean lady, whose disinheritance, it is said, caused her to turn to leftist ideologies. Presumably she was able to indoctrinate her husband along the same lines, and reports have it that Fortuny and other Communists were frequent visitors at the Arbenz home. Above all, Arbenz was a sincere and devoted Guatemalan nationalist, determined to refashion society in his country so that modernization could take place. And he would not tolerate any opposition.

In his inaugural address President Arbenz promised his countrymen that he would lead them "forward to a better Guatemala"—a modern capitalistic society, economically independent, and a model democracy with "greater well-being and prosperity" for its citizens. To achieve these objectives, he listened attentively to the recommendations made by a group of experts from the International Bank for Reconstruction and Development, who, at the behest of his predecessor, had conducted a three-month survey during the summer of 1950. As might be expected, the IBRD mission had a great deal to say about agricultural reforms. It felt that the government should stimulate coffee production as a means of financing further diversification of agriculture. To this end, Guatemala should consider the reorganization of the *Fincas Nacionales* and have them serve as model experiments that private coffee growers might imitate. The *Instituto Agropecuario Nacional,* in the meantime, should encourage widespread agricultural research, INFOP should attempt to control agricultural planning, and the government should take steps to improve marketing and credit facilities for small farmers. By developing the Pacific coast area Guatemala could assure herself a cheaper and more abundant food supply. Moreover, something should be done about improving the productivity of the highland Indians, by teaching them progressive methods or by attracting them to areas where they might increase their productivity and their income levels. These suggestions, and others made by foreign experts, were seriously considered and at least partially implemented in the controversial agrarian reform law of 1952, which we shall discuss subsequently.

The IBRD mission made other recommendations as well, 77 of them in all. As a result, INFOP expanded its operations into agriculture. In August 1951 INFOP bought $400,000 worth of heavy equipment to clear 600,000 acres of private land that the government hoped to make more productive. And in industry it contributed handsomely to the establishment of the first paper mill and plywood plant in Central America. That was in the fall of 1951. Although privately owned, the plant was largely financed by the government. Upon the recommendation of the IBRD mission the national airlines (*Aviateca*) were put under an autonomous agency for greater efficiency and profit. A similar suggestion was made with respect to the foreign insurance companies, but the Arbenz government received no cooperation from them. The experts further suggested that Guatemala perfect its transportation and communication system, but that the International Railways of Central America (IRCA) should remain in the hands of its present owners, limiting government intervention to the control of rates. The mission also approved of the 1947 industrial development law with its incentives to private investors, both foreign and domestic, a proposal agreed to by Arbenz providing foreign investors would be willing to share profits equitably with Guatemala.

On June 17, 1952, the Guatemalan legislature passed the agrarian reform law, unquestionably the most crucial piece of legislation enacted during the Arbenz years.[13] Although the law was basically similar to its Mexican counterpart, and even milder in some respects, its implementation and political implications were such that it contributed to the downfall of Jacobo Arbenz only slightly more than two years later. To Guatemalan reformers of that day, desperately in a hurry to achieve the millennium, the *Ley Agraria* was the panacea for the ills of the country, the key to economic progress and

[13] Nathan L. Whetten, *Guatemala—The Land and the People* (New Haven, 1961), pp. 152-66, an excellent discussion of the law and the problems it created.

a frontal assault on an antiquated land tenure system that was inefficient, wasteful, and inhuman. The constitution of 1945 had prepared the ground for this law; Arévalo the politician had approached the problem obliquely; and now Arbenz the military man ordered the attack—the shortest distance between two points was a straight line.

As in Mexico's case, the agrarian program came under the exclusive jurisdiction of the president; there could be no appeal to the courts. Aimed at large holdings (those over 223 acres), and especially unused lands, the law permitted the government to expropriate property either in the name of the state or in behalf of eligible recipients, with indemnification provided in the form of bonds bearing different maturity dates, but not to exceed 25 years. The rate of payment would be based on the recorded assessed value of the property on May 9, 1952. Land expropriated from private parties in the name of the state, as well as plots from the *Fincas Nacionales,* were to be leased to a recipient for his lifetime, and providing he paid annually 3 per cent of his crop's value. It has been estimated that 86 per cent of the lands expropriated by Arbenz fell into this category. Other expropriations could be transferred on a permanent basis with an annual payment of 5 per cent of the harvest's value. Unlike the Mexican system, grantees had freedom to rent their lands under certain conditions.

The bureaucracy involved was extensive: a National Agrarian Department, a National Agrarian Council, an agrarian commission for each department, and local committees at the municipal level. A National Agrarian Bank was authorized to supply credit to farmers at a reasonable level, a most constructive feature of the program when we consider the hardships experienced by small farmers in surviving until harvest time while paying interest rates ranging from 3.2 per cent to 12.6 per cent a month, according to a study conducted by the *Instituto Indigenista.*

In such a program, of course, the nature of the personnel chosen by the executive would be crucial, and it would seem that many of Arbenz' appointees were honest and competent, sincerely dedicated to uplifting and educating the landless Indians. But the heavy political orientation of the program—the unlimited authority of the president, the annual payments to the state, the prerogatives given labor in the selection of local committeemen, the virtual exclusion of the landowners' viewpoint—created a situation in which avowed Communists could distort the program to their advantage. Arbenz could not ignore their willingness to serve and their usefulness in carrying out the agrarian reforms, whatever their real motives may have been. Fiercely resisted by local landholders and foreign corporations, the agrarian reform was thrown off its tracks. Without adequate preparation, it went into high gear and became a political issue, no longer a genuine reform movement.

The landowners had legitimate grievances concerning the law and its implementation, for they had virtually no voice in the program. The "landless" and their national benefactors were in complete control of the situation—the pendulum had swung to the other extreme. When the landowners appealed to the courts in early 1953 and obtained an injunction, the Guatemalan legislature dismissed the four "unpatriotic" judges of the Supreme Court who dared challenge the constitutionality of the Law. Arbenz' military power, of course, had much to do with this; so did nationalistic feeling in Guatemala, with the Communists—an articulate and vociferous handful—riding the crest of the wave. Some landowners refused compliance with that part of the law which expropriated the workers' dwellings on their *fincas,* and the *finquero's* violent reaction, however justifiable under the conditions, merely begat more violence from his enemies. Frustration and anger on both sides gave the ultranationalists and Communists the advantage in the mounting emotional crisis. Through their control of news media they whipped up revolutionary sentiment throughout Guatemala. At their instigation mobs of Indians moved into lands and squatted on them without any legal authorization, and the rule of law began to break down, giving way to anarchy.

The issue of "imperialism," however, overshadowed the domestic struggle between Left and Right and gave the minority of Communists their best chance to sound off. Local oligarchs were bad enough, but at least they were Guatemalans, cut from the same fabric; you just used the horsewhip on them, as President Barrios had once said. It was easier and far more popular to focus attention on the outsider as an obstacle to the October "Revolution": the North American owners of utilities (*Empresa Eléctrica*) who restricted out put because they preferred a large profit from a small volume of business and did not share Guatemalans' vision of the brighter future; the International Railways of Central America, also representing Northern investors, which was more interested in monopoly than in service to the country; and the real villain, the United Fruit Company, a heavy investor in the other two organizations, which refused to abide by the nation's laws and pay its workers a decent wage. There was, of course, a great deal of economic nonsense in these charges, but inflamed minds were unable to appreciate it, especially when the company owners buttressed the prevailing stereotype with unenlightened actions and indiscreet remarks that provided grist for the propaganda mill.

The trouble between UFCO and the Guatemalan government had begun in the late forties when company officials rejected outright Arévalo's request to renegotiate a contract on a more equitable, long-term basis. The situation went from bad to worse under Arbenz as aggressive labor leaders challenged the American companies and the government espoused the workers' cause. In IRCA's case, for example, the government seized its assets on April 1, 1953, on the ground that it had not paid charity taxes, a pretext obviously intended to force management's hand. *La Frutera* also fought the demand for higher wages to banana workers, arguing that they were already receiving three times those of the regular Guatemalan laborer.[14] But three times nothing was hardly the solution that labor leaders were seeking; the important thing was a breakthrough with the foreign companies that would strengthen unionism throughout Guatemala and thus raise the general wage level of the country. The stakes were large, and very few people were in a compromising mood. The Communists, as might be expected, watched for and blew up every one of the company's miscues. They had an easy time of it, of course; it was not difficult to be a conspirator under those conditions.

The Agrarian law brought matters to a head. UFCO argued that its uncultivated lands were necessary as potential reserves to protect itself against disease, which afflicted the industry frequently, or disastrous hurricanes such as the one that destroyed the year's crop at Tiquisate in 1951, all perfectly legitimate objections, to be sure. Often

[14] Martz, *op. cit.*, pp. 47-52, treats this subject objectively.

overlooked, the real problem was that UFCO possessed valuable lands in western Guatemala where the Arbenz regime hoped to satisfy the food requirements of its people, just as the IBRD had suggested. That is where the bulk of the land expropriated from UFCO lay. When expropriation took place, the question was then how much would be paid for the land. The company argued that the actual worth of the land was $15,854,849, yet for tax purposes it had been assessed at $609,572. The actual value, in other words, was 26 times its assessed value.[15] And since UFCO could not take the matter to court, it asked the State Department to protect its interests.

On March 23, 1953, the United States government officially took up the defense of American interests in Guatemala by requesting adequate compensation. Guatemala replied two months later that she was legally entitled to seize property, only to receive a stronger request from authorities in Washington. The die had been cast. Yankeephobia as well as a sense of humiliation and frustration swept over the Land of the Quetzal. Once its government was committed, UFCO showed no willingness whatsover to compromise, and the Communists had a heyday in the propaganda field. On April 20, 1954, the United States government determined, using UFCO figures, that the official reparation should be $15,854,849. The spirit of Frederick Chatfield was still alive in Central America.

The showdown was not long in coming. In early 1954 Castillo Armas was already training his troops in their Honduran exile, six months prior to the movement of "liberation." The knowledge of impending invasion touched off a reign of terror in Guatemala that brought the "Revolution" to a sudden halt. Like a man obsessed, Colonel Arbenz grasped at all straws to save his regime. Whereas previously he had scrupulously adhered to constitutionalism, permitting the press to speak out against him, he now resorted to the methods of the guardhouse, and at this point his followers began to drop by the wayside. And though the reports of atrocities and torture may be discounted heavily, there is no question that the regime was desperate and that Guatemalans chose to believe those reports. They were no longer willing to support a government that might lead them toward Communism. Perhaps they were just rationalizing their

[15] Whetten, op. cit., pp. 159-60.

unwillingness to give their lives for a revolution that could not possibly succeed against the determined opposition of the United States.

And the writing was on the wall for everyone to see. At Caracas in March 1954 in the Tenth Inter-American Conference, John Foster Dulles threw the entire weight of his country behind an anti-Communist resolution. And pass it did; Guatemala alone voted against it, while the large countries of Mexico and Argentina abstained. But Dulles' victory for democracy and freedom was indeed a shallow one. Hoping for economic assistance, Latin Americans had gone along with their rich neighbor, but they were not proud of their action—in fact, they were probably humiliated by it—nor did they feel that it was really necessary. Throughout Latin America the conviction grew that "dollar diplomacy" had once again returned to the New World and that the United States was not genuinely interested in advancing Latin American national aspirations.

In the meantime the Guatemalan government repeatedly denied the charges of "international Communism" and countered with the accusation that it was a smokescreen thrown up to permit American interests to satisfy their greed, despoiling national resources without restraint or respect for the country in question. On May Day, 1954, Communists and ultranationalists hammered away at this same theme. By May 17, thousands of UFCO workers were on strike. They gained about 85 per cent of their demands within a month's time.

And the situation grew steadily worse. To protect himself against the rumored invasion, Arbenz sought weapons from behind the Iron Curtain—the United States, of course, was not about to give him any. Then, on May 17, the world was electrified by the news that the Alfhem was on the high seas with a shipload of arms she had taken on in Stettin, Poland. The Alfhem reached Puerto Barrios and disposed of her cargo. This provided the United States with the excuse for sending additional weapons to Honduras and Nicaragua, hoping thus to redress the balance of power in Central America. The involvement of Guatemalan agents in the Honduran strike of that year was also a contributing factor. Even Arbenz realized that perhaps he had gone too far in defying the United States, and he suggested a personal interview with President Eisenhower, a meeting that might have had interesting results if it had taken place. But the United States government showed no interest in the suggestion; it would not negotiate the issue of Communism.

And so President Jacobo Arbenz fell from power on June 27, 1954, because of the pressures from without and from within. The Guatemalan military, alarmed at the possibility that the Communists might arm the peasants, arranged for the ouster. The American Ambassador John Peurifoy played a key role in the negotiations that brought about the cease-fire in Guatemala, adding to his impressive record as a trouble-shooter in Communist areas. The forces of "liberation" under the popular Carlos Castillo Armas marched into the capital triumphantly and for the next three years tried their hand at controlling the Guatemalan "Revolution"—a record we have already examined.

It is perhaps no coincidence that Yankeephobia and Communism spread simultaneously throughout Latin America after 1954. No serious student of Latin American affairs questions the fact that Communists held key positions in the Arbenz government. To interpret the Guatemalan "Revolution" solely in those terms, however, is to deny ourselves full insight concerning the problems and aspirations of those countries. The idea of "nationalism," no matter how tenuous and difficult it is to describe or how ridiculous and absurd its manifestations may be, is a vital force in Latin America, as well as elsewhere in the world. We must learn to reckon with it and direct it into safe channels. This, it will be recalled, was the imaginative objective of President Kennedy's Alliance for Progress. It recognized that the depressed conditions of Latin American life had to be solved, thus eliminating a further breeding ground for Communism and permitting the healthy development of democratic institutions. Although the problems are formidable, perhaps even insurmountable, a great democratic nation has a world-wide and moral obligation to make the attempt. In so doing, we shall also be serving our own best interests.

Moreover, it would be folly to assume that democratic ideals are recent innovations in Latin America. Our review of Central American history should remind us that liberalism, though frustrated at every turn by various obstacles, is a deep-rooted force in that area. It should be cultivated and encouraged by the United States, an American nation which has stood and fought for those same ideals over the decades. But words are not enough. We must prove our sincerity of purpose with constructive and imaginative measures, such as those embodied in the *Alianza*. To do otherwise will just foster the spread of Communism throughout Latin America. It serves no useful purpose—certainly not ours—to blame the Communists for everything, thus absolving ourselves from any responsibility for the conditions that gave them a foothold in Guatemala. An intelligent man should admit his mistake, accept responsibility for it, and then see to it that it never happens again—and the same applies to nations.

There is no denying that President John Fitzgerald Kennedy had a tremendous impact on the Latin American mind. Admiration for him is still very much alive throughout Latin America; "If only Kennedy had lived" is a common utterance that many of us have heard frequently. The implication is that his successor to the presidency does not share Kennedy's democratic premises, that they have been lost sight of in the emotionalism of the Cuban crisis. The emphasis is again on the military solution, the acceptance of military regimes throughout Latin America which presumably will hold the fort against the Communist invasion. If my analysis of the nationalistic idea is valid, the present policy of the United States will inevitably frustrate and undermine our natural allies throughout Latin America, the moderate democratic elements, and force them into the neutralist camp. As in Guatemala, the ultranationalists will return to power and in one way or another will compel American business interests—if our European allies have not completely replaced us by then—to accept their laws on expropriation, investment, and so on. The military solution may satisfy our immediate fears and strategic requirements, but it contains the seeds of its own destruction: the support of groups inimical to *Alianza* objectives, the pseudo-democratic structures that will arise; the pump-priming of economies that will outgrow their present suits, and the strengthening of elements that will favor independence from United States' control.

It would be wiser, and more profitable for ourselves, to get the Alliance for Progress back on the road which President Kennedy intended. In the long run, and despite many serious obstacles, it would cost us less and at the same time undermine the extremists throughout Latin America, including the Communists.

Interest in Central America has always been keen among English-speaking people, especially since the independence of that area from Spain. The economic resources and potential of Middle America attracted Englishmen and later North Americans; the discovery that the Mayas had created a separate and distinct civilization fascinated scholars; the possibility of constructing a passageway across Central America led to an intense rivalry between the United States and Great Britain; the strategic and economic importance of the area to its Northern neighbor sustained the interest; and finally the implications of the "Revolution" have again focused the world's attention on the central portion of the Western Hemisphere. Let us therefore select and examine some of the major works that reflect this interest and that the curious reader may consult with profit.

For those who would like to compile a more extensive bibliography, I suggest the following works: Robin A. Humphreys, *Latin American History: A Guide to the Literature in English* (London, 1958); P. Lee Phillips, *A List of Books, Magazine Articles, and Maps Relating to Central America* (Washington, 1902); Henry Grattan Doyle, "A Tentative Bibliography of the Belles-Lettres of the Republics of Central America," the last essay in A. Curtis Wilgus, ed., *The Caribbean: The Central American Area* (Gainesville, 1961); William J. Griffith, "The Historiography of Central America Since 1830," *Hispanic American Historical Review*, XL (1960), 548-69; Julio Adolfo Rey, "Revolution and Liberation: A Review of Recent Literature on the Guatemalan Situation," *Hispanic American Historical Review*, XXXVIII (1958), 239-55; Irene

Zimmerman, A *Guide to Current Latin American Periodicals: Humanities and Social Sciences* (Gainesville, 1961); Nathan L. Whetten, *Guatemala—The Land and the People* (New Haven, 1961), pp. 373-87; and Franklin D. Parker, *The Central American Republics* (London, 1964), pp. 319-34, as well as the excellent discussion of references in appropriate sections of the text. *The Hispanic American Report* (Stanford University), founded in November 1948, and the *Handbook of Latin American Studies* (Library of Congress, The Hispanic Foundation) are both indispensable guides to the literature published in the last two decades.

The father of Mayan studies in the United States was John Lloyd Stephens, an American diplomat with an exceptional writing talent, who published two volumes entitled *Incidents of Travel in Central America, Chiapas, and Yucatán* (New York, 1841); in 1949 R. L. Predmore edited another edition (New Brunswick, New Jersey). He was the first to recognize that the Mayas had a civilization of their own, a thesis subsequent scholars were able to substantiate. Victor Wolfgang von Hagen's *Maya Explorer* (Norman, 1947) is an excellent biography of Stephens, who, incidentally, was a good friend of Chatfield (perhaps that is why Stephens did not mention Chatfield's political machinations in the text of the work). Ephraim George Squier, in his works *Nicaragua* (2 vols., New York, 1852) and *Notes on Central America* (New York, 1855), provided accurate information on the Indians of the three center states. Hubert Howe Bancroft and his research team summarized the various studies on Central American Indians in their monumental work, *The Native Races of the Pacific States of North America* (5 vols., San Francisco, 1874-75).

Thanks to the support of the Peabody Museum, the Smithsonian Institution, the Middle American Research Institute (Tulane University), and the Carnegie Institution, only to name a few, twentieth-century scholarship on the Mayas has been brilliant. The list of contributors is too long to permit mention of all the significant studies. The following are samples of the field: Herbert J. Spinden, *A Study of Maya Art* (Cambridge, Mass., 1913) and his *Ancient Civilizations of Mexico and Central America* (New York, 1917); J. Eric S. Thompson, *The Rise and Fall of Maya Civilization* (Norman, 1954); Sylvanus G. Morley, *The Ancient Maya*, edited by George W. Brainerd (Palo Alto, 1956); Tatiana Proskouriakoff, *A Study of Classic Maya Sculpture*; Alfred Kidder II and Carlos Samayoa Chinchilla, *The Art of the Ancient Maya* (New York, 1959); and Sylvanus G. Morley and Delia Goetz's translation of

Adrián Recinos' *Popul Vuh: The Sacred Book of the Ancient Quiché Maya* (Norman, 1950).

Despite its weaknesses by modern standards, Hubert Howe Bancroft's *History of Central America* (3 vols., San Francisco, 1882-87) is still the best general reference in English for the colonial period and for the nineteenth century up to 1882. It is influenced by the prejudices of its colonial sources and by the nineteenth-century liberal viewpoint. A well-written and shorter account is Alcée Fortier and John Rose Ficklen's *Central America and Mexico* (Philadelphia, 1907). For the Conquest see the Cortes Society's S. J. Mackie translation of Pedro de Alvarado's *An Account of the Conquest of Guatemala in 1524*; the penetrating and thorough study of the modern historian Robert S. Chamberlain, *The Conquest and Colonization of Honduras, 1502-1550* (Washington, 1953); and the translation by Harry Weston Van Dyke of Ricardo Fernández Guardia's *History of the Discovery and Conquest of Costa Rica* (New York, 1913), the work of an able *Tico* scholar who captured the spirit of the times.

The accounts and studies of the later colonial period, though not numerous, have been of high quality. Thanks to the Smithsonian Institution, there is a translation of Antonio Vázquez de Espinosa's *Compendium and Description of the West Indies* (Washington, 1942) by Charles Upson Clark, which, coupled with Thomas Gage's *The English-American: A New Survey of the West Indies, 1648*, edited by Arthur P. Newton (London, 1928), provides us with contemporary viewpoints during the much neglected seventeenth century. For the following century we have John Cockburn's *A Journey Over Land, from the Gulf of Honduras to the Great South-Sea* (London, 1740); Volume I of Alexander von Humboldt's *Personal Narrative of Travels to the Equinoctial Regions of America* (London, 1872); and Domingo Juarros, *A Statistical and Commercial History of the Kingdom of Guatemala* (London, 1823), which was translated by John Baily. In the *Iberoamericana* series of the University of California (Berkeley), Lesley Byrd Simpson has studied the forced labor system of Central America, not to mention his now classic work on the *Encomienda in New Spain*, which first appeared in 1938 (Berkeley). Also in the economic field are the following excellent articles: Troy S. Floyd, "The Guatemalan Merchants, the Government, and the *Provincianos*, 1750-1800," *Hispanic American Historical Review*, XLI (1961), and Robert S. Smith, "Indigo Production and Trade in Colonial Guatemala," *Hispanic American Historical Review*, XXXIX (1959), and "Origins of the Consulado of Guatemala," *Hispanic Ameri* can *Historical Review*, XXVI (1946). Robert Jones Shafer, *The Economic Societies in the Spanish World* (1763-1821) (Syracuse, 1958), is heavily weighted toward Guatemalan events. John Tate Lanning of Duke University has written definitive studies on the intellectual renaissance during the late Bourbon period in Central America: *Academic Culture in the Spanish Colonies* (New York, 1940), *The University in the Kingdom of Guatemala* (Ithaca, 1955), and *The Eighteenth-Century Enlightenment in the University of San Carlos de Guatemala* (Ithaca, 1956).

For the pre-independence period is the well-written and thorough study by Louis E. Bumgartner, *José del Valle of Central America* (Durham, 1963), which concentrates on the activity of that famous *provinciano* up to the year 1824, the last seven years of Valle's life receiving less emphasis. Another study of the Honduran savant, originally a Master's thesis at the University of Illinois, is that of Franklin D. Parker, *José Cecilio del Valle and the Establishment of the Central American Confederation* (Tegucigalpa, 1954), which does a good job of digesting the printed documentation and major Spanish works of the period; it is especially valuable for the last years of Valle's life.

The story of the Central American Republic has fascinated North American scholars. In addition to the above-mentioned works of Bumgartner and Parker, there are those by Robert S. Chamberlain, *Francisco Morazán, Champion of Central American Federation* (Coral Gables, 1950), a solid synthesis of works in Spanish written on Morazán up to that time; Harold Bond Field, "The Central-American Federation, a Political Study, 1826-1839" (unpublished Ph.D. thesis, University of Chicago, 1942), which contains the best analysis of the 1824 constitution that I have seen; Francis Merriman Stanger, "National Origins in Central America," *Hispanic American Historical Review*, XII (1932), which highlights the divisive forces of geography, race, and history; Robert S. Smith, "Financing the Central American Federation, 1821-1838," *Hispanic American Historical Review*, XLIII (1963), a key contribution to that subject; Mary W. Williams, "The Ecclesiastical Policy of Francisco Morazán and the Other Central American Liberals," *Hispanic American Historical Review*, III (1920), which considers the vindictive actions toward the clergy as a prime cause for the failure of the Republic; William Joyce Griffith, "Juan Galindo, Central American Chauvinist," *Hispanic American Historical Review*, XL (1960), which takes a dim view of that foreigner's actions in Central America; Ian Graham, "Juan Galindo, Enthusiast," *Estudios de Cultura Maya*, III

(Mexico, 1963), which in turn questions Griffith's fairness and is impressed with Galindo's contribution to Mayan studies—Graham is an Englishman, I should add; Thomas L. Karnes, "The Origins of Costa Rican Federalism," *The Americas*, XV (1959), a perceptive study; and my own study, *The Livingston Codes in the Guatemalan Crisis of 1837-1838*. Professor Griffith of Tulane University will shortly publish a book on the colonization efforts of foreigners, which should be an outstanding contribution to the study of the Republic and the post-1839 years.

In addition there are three major works that extend beyond the period of the Republic because of the nature of the themes they treat. Thomas L. Karnes, *The Failure of Union: Central America, 1824-1960* (Chapel Hill, 1961), is an excellent over-all view of unionist effort from the time of the Republic to the present economic program; Mary P. Holleran, *Church and State in Guatemala* (New York, 1949), is valuable for its documentation and political insights concerning this touchy issue from the time of the Republic to the years of Arévalo; and my study, *A Palmerstonian Diplomat in Central America: Frederick Chatfield, Esq.* (Tucson, 1964), deals with the Republic's final years and Chatfield's political maneuvers up to 1852 and perhaps may help to settle the heated controversy concerning the nature of England's actions in Central America during the first half of the nineteenth century, referred to on pp. 375-77 of the above-mentioned work.

The theme of international rivalry in Central America has also been a popular one among English-speaking authors. Mary W. Williams, *Anglo-American Isthmian Diplomacy, 1815-1915* (Washington, 1916), is still the standard authority on that subject; Ira D. Travis, *British Rule in Central America: or a Sketch of Mosquito History* (Ann Arbor, 1895), and *The History of the Clayton-Bulwer Treaty* (Ann Arbor, 1900), are pioneer studies that still can be read with profit; William O. Scroggs, *Filibusters and Financiers* (New York, 1916) has stood up well, despite many challengers, as the classic on William Walker's actions in Central America. On the controversial Belize Question we can only say that the battle has just begun. Among the important works on this controversy, as well as studies of British Honduras (the Guatemalans insist that its name is Belize) are: Robin A. Humphreys, *The Diplomatic History of British Honduras, 1638-1901* (London, 1961); David A. G. Waddell, *British Honduras: a Historical and Contemporary Survey* (London, 1961); William J. Bianchi, *Belize: the Controversy between Guatemala and Great Britain over the Territory of British Honduras in Central America* (New York, 1959); Louis M. Bloomfield, *The British Honduras-Guate-*

mala Dispute (Toronto, 1953); and Wayne M. Clegern's articles "New Light on the Belize Dispute," *American Journal of International Law*, LII (1958) and "A Guatemalan Defense of the British Honduras Boundary of 1859," *Hispanic American Historical Review*, XL (1960), which constitute a scholarly rebuttal to the English viewpoint. His impending monograph on British Honduras will be a welcomed contribution to the field. For printed documentation on this subject, as well as a list of the major accounts of travelers in nineteenth-century Central America, see my *Palmerstonian Diplomat*, pp. 374-75. Gordon Ireland, *Boundaries, Possessions and Conflicts in Central and North America and the Caribbean* (Cambridge, Mass., 1941), is indispensable for the study of the frequent territorial disputes among Central American countries.

For the period from 1871 to 1918 the literature in English on political matters is adequate though by no means exhaustive. Amateur historian and Presbyterian missionary Paul Burgess wrote *Justo Rufino Barrios: A Biography* (Philadelphia, 1926), a surprisingly penetrating analysis except in those sections where he simply lists laws passed, without much comment; his discussion of authorities is excellent, revealing a critical mind. On the subject of Barrios and unionism see the appropriate chapter in Karnes, *The Failure of Union,* and the more recent monograph by John D. Martz, *Justo Rufino Barrios and Central American Union* (Gainesville, 1963), which profited from the use of American diplomatic documents. For a semifictional account of the "Great Reformer" see Alice Raine, *Eagle of Guatemala: Justo Rufino Barrios* (New York, 1941). By far the best coverage for the entire period is Professor Dana G. Munro, *The Five Republics of Central America* (New York, 1918) which treats the social, economic, political, and diplomatic aspects of the Central American experience; his treatment of the pre-1871 years is limited, however.

As might be expected, North American historians have been much concerned with the policy of their country in Middle America. Thanks to Dana G. Munro's *Intervention and Dollar Diplomacy in the Caribbean, 1900-1921* (Princeton, 1964), we now have a comprehensive view of the entire policy; the facts are all there, but the reader does not have to accept Professor Munro's interpretation of them. Among the scholarly studies on various aspects of this subject we should include: Isaac J. Cox, *Nicaragua and the United States, 1909-1927* (Boston, 1927); Roscoe R. Hill, *Fiscal Intervention in Nicaragua* (New York, 1933), and his *American Marines in Nicaragua, 1912-1915* (Washington, 1942); Thomas A. Bailey, "Interest in a Nicaraguan Canal," *Hispanic American Historical*

Review, XVI (1936); Philip M. Brown, "American Diplomacy in Central America," *American Political Science Review,* VI (Supplement, 1912); Manley O. Hudson, "The Central American Court of Justice," *American Journal of International Law,* XXVI (1932); and the perceptive articles by Joseph O. Baylen, "American Intervention in Nicaragua, 1909-33: an Appraisal of Objectives and Results," *Southwestern Social Science Quarterly,* XXXV (1954), and "Sandino: Patriot or Bandit," *Hispanic American Historical Review,* XXXI (1951). Harold Norman Denny, *Dollars for Bullets* (New York, 1929), shows what a journalist did with this story, and Rafael de Nogales, *The Looting of Nicaragua* (New York, 1928), is typical of the voluminous and passionate output of Latin Americans on this topic. Juan José Arévalo's *The Shark and the Sardines* (New York, 1961) chooses the Nicaraguan interventions of the early twentieth century to illustrate the incompatibility of the Americas, Anglo-Saxon and Latin. Written shortly after the fall of Arbenz, it reflects the frustration and disillusionment with the United States that pervaded Latin America in the late fifties. Undoubtedly, this book, read by millions throughout the world, made Arévalo's comeback in Guatemalan politics a virtual impossibility, stigmatizing him as a Red.

Since the publication of Munro's book on Central America (1918), and with very few exceptions, the nonhistorian has taken over the task of describing developments in Central America. Karnes' work on unionism, and the diplomatic studies mentioned above, are the exceptions. A professor of economics and political science, Chester Lloyd Jones of the University of Wisconsin wrote an excellent treatise entitled *Costa Rica and Civilization in the Caribbean* (Madison, 1935), and followed this by another one, *Guatemala, Past and Present* (Minneapolis, 1940), considered the best study on that country for its wealth of information on social, economic, and political trends. It is, of course, somewhat dated now. John and Mavis Biesanz, *Costa Rican Life* (New York, 1944), the work of sociologists, provides an excellent view of the *Ticos'* daily life; William S. Stokes, *Honduras: An Area Study in Government* (Madison, 1950), is excellent for the analysis of the political system and the Carías regime; John Parke Young, *Central American Currency and Finance* (Princeton, 1925), is a pioneer on that subject and on economic developments in general. See also Kenneth Grubb, *Religion in Central America* (London, 1937), and George Cheever Shattuck, *A Medical Survey of the Republic of Guatemala* (Washington, 1938). On the United Fruit Company the literature both pro and con includes: Charles David Kepner, *Social Aspects of the Banana Industry* (New York, 1936);

Kepner and Jay Henry Soothill, *The Banana Empire* (New York, 1935); Charles Morrow Wilson, *Empire in Green and Gold* (New York, 1947); and Stacy May and Galo Plaza, *The United Fruit Company in Latin America* (Washington, 1958).

On contemporary Central America—that is, since 1945—the literature is overwhelming; again, most of it is by non-historians. *The Hispanic American Report*, edited by Ronald Hilton of Stanford University, contains the best coverage, month by month, of events that have transpired in Central America since 1948. It, along with the New York *Times*, especially good in times of crises, are the main references I have used in my evaluation of the present scene. Among the general accounts of the area the following should be mentioned: John D. Martz, *Central America: The Crisis and the Challenge* (Chapel Hill, 1959), which presents a lively, though pessimistic, account of political developments in Central America and Panama; Thorsten V. Kalijarvi, *Central America: Land of Lords and Lizards* (Princeton and elsewhere, 1962), valuable for its geographic and economic information, not for its historical presentation; and Franklin D. Parker's *The Central American Republics* (London, 1964), easily the best treatment of the many-faceted experience of Central America, briefly describing the political events.

On the present common market Karnes provides the background. Joseph Pincus, *The Central American Common Market* (Washington, 1962), is authoritative on the economic possibilities of union; Frank L. Keller, "ODECA: Common Market Experiment in an Under-Developed Area," *Journal of Inter-American Studies*, V (1963), covers the movement with broad strokes; James L. Busey, "Central American Union: The Latest Attempt," *The Western Political Quarterly*, XIV (1961) supplements Karnes' treatment of the subject; Julian S. Duncan, "Demographic Factors and Economic Integration in Central America," *Journal of Inter-American Studies*, V (1963) contains vital statistics, as does Robert S. Smith's "Population and Economic Growth in Central America," *Economic Development and Cultural Change*, X (1962). See also Norman J. Padelford, "Cooperation in the Central American Region: the Organization of Central States," *International Organization*, XI (1957) and Charles G. Fenwick, "The Organization of Central American States," *The American Journal of International Law*, XLVI (1952).

For the area as a whole the following works are useful: Richard N. Adams, *Cultural Surveys of Panama-Nicaragua-Guatemala-El Salvador-Honduras* (Washington, 1957), dealing with socio-cultural factors; The United Nations, *The Population of Central America (Including Mexico)*,

1950-1980 (New York, 1954); Archie Fairly Carr, *High Jungles and Low* (Gainesville, 1953), on natural history; C. L. Dozier, *Indigenous Tropical Agriculture in Central America* (Washington, 1958); Evangelical Foreign Missions Association, *Protestant Missions in Latin America: A Statistical Survey* (Washington, 1961); United States Bureau of Foreign Commerce, *Investment in Central America* (Washington, 1956); and United States Bureau of Labor Statistics, *Labor Law and Practice in Honduras* (Washington, 1961), *Labor Law and Practice in Guatemala* (Washington, 1962), and *Labor Law and Practice in Cost Rica* (Washington, 1962). The Pan American Union in Washington has also put out copies of the various constitutions: Costa Rica (1951), El Salvador (1953), Nicaragua (1954), Guatemala (1956), and Honduras (1958). Preston E. James, *Latin America* (New York, 1950), devotes considerable space to the geography of the five countries.

There are, moreover, detailed studies dealing with various aspects of life in each of the Central American states. The following are indicative: International Bank for Reconstruction and Development, *The Economic Development of Guatemala* (Baltimore, 1951), and *The Economic Development of Nicaragua* (Baltimore, 1953); Vera Kelsey and Lilly de Jongh Osborne, *Four Keys to Guatemala* (2d ed., New York, 1961), and the latter's *Four Keys to El Salvador* (New York, 1956), delightful for their folkloric content; Nathan L. Whetten, *Guatemala—The Land and the People* (New Haven, 1961), based on the 1950 census and subsequent research; John H. Adler, *et al.*, *Public Finance and Economic Development in Guatemala* (Palo Alto, 1952); Frederick J. Tower, *Basic Data on the Economy of Honduras* (Washington, 1961); Vincent Checchi, *et al.*, *Honduras: A Problem in Economic Development* (New York, 1959); Henry C. Wallich, *et al.*, *Public Finance in a Developing Country: El Salvador—A Case Study* (Cambridge, Mass., 1951); Willy John Feuerlein, *Proposals for the Further Economic Development of El Salvador* (New York, 1954), and Berthold Frank Hoselitz, *Industrial Development of El Salvador* (New York, 1954), both United Nations studies; George P. Turner, *An Analysis of the Economy of El Salvador, April, 1961* (Los Angeles, 1961); William Vogt, *The Population of El Salvador and Its Natural Resources* (New York, 1946); James L. Busey, *Notes on Costa Rican Democracy* (Boulder, 1962); Philip L. Wagner, *Nicoya, a Cultural Geography* (Berkeley, 1958); Stacy May, *et al.*, *Costa Rica: A Study in Economic Development* (New York, 1952); Charles P. Loomis, *et al.*, *Turrialba: Social Systems and the Introduction of Change* (Glencoe, Ill., 1953); Robert E. Nunley, *The Distribution of Population in Costa Rica* (Washington, 1960); and Harry Kantor, *The Costa Rican Election of 1953: A Case Study* (Gainesville, 1958).

As might be expected, the Guatemalan "Revolution" has been the subject of countless pages, not all of them well digested. Among the leading works are these: Leo A. Suslow, *Aspects of Social Reforms in Guatemala, 1944-1949,* and Archer C. Bush, *Organized Labor in Guatemala, 1944-1949,* both published in mimeograph form by the Colgate Press in Hamilton, New York, in 1949 and 1950 respectively—excellent on their subjects; Kalman H. Silvert, *A Study in Government: Guatemala* (New Orleans, 1954), a masterly evaluation of the 1945 constitution, the political context in which it was framed, and its implementation—moreover, he examines the Communist threat objectively; Samuel Guy Inman, *A New Day in Guatemala, A Study of the Present Social Revolution* (Wilton, Conn., 1951), quite definitely favorable to the "Revolution"; Ronald M. Schneider, *Communism in Guatemala, 1944-1954* (New York, 1958), the best on this subject though a balanced treatment would have been more satisfying for the reasons I have expressed in the text; Daniel James, *Red Design for the Americas: Guatemalan Prelude* (New York, 1954), which at least recognizes the force of nationalism—his treatment of Arévalo is typical of the "conspiracy" approach; John D. Martz, *Communist Infiltration in Guatemala* (New York, 1956); and Robert J. Alexander, *Communism in Latin America* (New Brunswick, 1957). See also the "official" views of the United States and British governments: *Intervention of International Communism in Guatemala* (Washington, 1954), *A Case History of Communist Penetration—Guatemala* (Washington, 1957), and *Report on Events Leading up to and Arising out of the Change of Régime in Guatemala* (London, 1954). Phillip B. Taylor, "The Guatemalan Affair: A Critique of United States Foreign Policy," *American Political Science Review,* L (1956), considering the time of writing, deserves to be congratulated for objectively analyzing our policy in Guatemala.

For a scholarly view we must not ignore the Latin writers, despite their passionate defense of the "Revolution" and excoriation of American intervention. Diego Córdoba, "Personalidad, obra, y paradigna de Juan José Arévalo," *Cuadernos Americanos,* CXIV (1961), is well worth perusing. Juan José Arévalo, *Escritos Políticos* (Guatemala, 1945), is valuable for an understanding of his objectives, provided we also understand the historical past of Guatemala; his *Anti-Komunismo en América Latina* (3rd ed., La Habana, 1960) is the "conspiracy" approach in reverse—Wall Street and its tool the State Department deliberately bringing down the "Revolution." Manuel Galich, *Del Pánico al Ataque* (Guatemala, 1949), are reminiscences of the Ubico period and his fall by a leading participant; his *Por qué lucha Guatemala* (Buenos Aires, 1956), is perhaps the best defense of Arévalo and Arbenz. Mario Méndez Montenegro, "La Revolución Guatemalteca," *Combate* (1959), is excellent for understanding the aims of the "Revolution." Guillermo Toriello, *La Batalla de Guatemala* (Mexico, 1955), is typical of the emotional literature by Latin Americans.

The impact of the "Revolution" on the Indian has intrigued anthropologists and sociologists of high calibre—such names as Oliver La Farge, Charles Wagley, Sol Tax and many others. See Whetten's *Guatemala* for an extensive bibliography. For the historian the following works are especially useful: Richard N. Adams, ed., *Political Changes in Guatemalan Indian Communities. A Symposium* (New Orleans, 1957), consisting of nine essays written by leading anthropologists who suggest that political policy and action are the media of the acculturation process; John Gillin, *Culture of Security in San Carlos: A Study of a Guatemalan Community of Indians and Ladinos* (New Orleans, 1951); Gillin and Kalman H. Silvert, "Ambiguities in Guatemala," *Foreign Affairs*, XXXIV (1955-56), which considers the Castillo Armas regime; Manning Nash, *Machine Age Maya: The Industrialization of a Guatemalan Community* (Glencoe, Ill., 1958); Ruben E. Reina, *Chinautla, a Guatemalan Indian Community* (New Orleans, 1960), and his "Political Crisis and Cultural Revitalization: the Guatemalan Case," *Human Organization*, XVII (1958-1959), which study the village in comparison with the capital; Elizabeth E. Hoyt, "The Indian Laborer on Guatemalan Coffee Fincas," *Inter-American Economic Affairs*, IX (1955), dealing with 50 farms, four of which belonged to the government; and stimulating articles by Richard F. Behrendt, "The Uprooted—A Guatemalan Sketch," *New Mexico Quarterly Review*, XIX (1949), dealing with the confused and dissatisfied Indian, and by Stokes Newbold, "Receptivity to Communist Fomented Agitation in Rural Guatemala," *Economic Development and Cultural Change*, V (1958-1959), demonstrating that there was no "ideological awakening" among the Indians, that they voted to fill their pocketbooks.

In short, the social sciences have been doing excellent work in the contemporary period, while the more conservative historians have abdicated the field to them, with but few exceptions.

INDEX

171

The Modern Nations in Historical Perspective